1001 WAYS TO BEAT THE DRAFT

by Tuli Kupferberg
and Robert Bashlow

GROVE PRESS, INC.   NEW YORK

AVEC APPROBATION,
ET PRIVILEGE
DU ROY.

The authors hereby acknowledge the contributions of the following: BB, EB, AD, RD, ee, GE, AG, NG, PG, PH, BK, DK, LK, OK, SK, DL, LM, GPO, PO, ES, HS, JS, TS, JW, KW

1. Grope J. Edgar Hoover in the silent halls of Congress.
2. Get thee to a nunnery.
3. Fly to the moon and refuse to come home.
4. Die.
5. Become Secretary of Defense.
6. Become Secretary of State.
7. Become Secretary of Health, Education and Welfare.
8. Show a li'l tit.
9. Castrate yourself.
10. Invent a time machine and go back to the 19th century.
11. Start to menstruate. (Better red than dead.)
12. Attempt to overthrow the Government of the United States by force and violence.
13. Advocate sexual freedom for children.
14. Shoot up for a day.
15. Refuse to speak to them at all.
16. Enroll at the Jefferson School of Social Science.
17. Replace your feet with wheels.
18. Rent a motel room with a ewe.
19. Rent a motel room with a ram.

20. Say you're crazy.
21. Say they're crazy.
22. Get muscular dystrophy when you're a kid.
23. Marry J. Edgar Hoover.
24. Take up residence in Albania.
25. Stretch yourself on a rack so that you become over 6½ feet tall.
26. Marry your mother.
27. Marry your father.
28. Blow up the Statue of Liberty.
29. Marry your sister.
30. Marry your brother.
31. Marry your daughter.
32. Join the Abraham Lincoln Brigade.
33. Marry your son.
34. Marry Lassie.
35. Marry President Johnson.
36. Marry Mao Tse-tung.

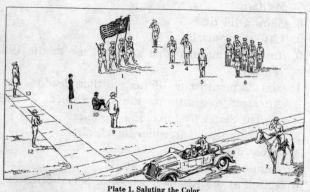

Plate 1. Saluting the Color

1. The colors and their guard.
2. Officer or soldier in uniform, not under arms, covered or uncovered.
3. Civilian, officer or soldier in civilian clothes, covered, fair weather.
4. Same as (3), rainy weather.
5. Civilian, officer or soldier in civilian clothes or athletic costume, uncovered.
6. Small detachment, armed with rifle non-commissioned officer in command.
7. Officer or soldier in uniform, mounted.
8. Driver and passenger of military vehicle in motion.
9-10. Ignorant or indifferent man and woman.
11. A lady saluting the color correctly (standing). She may place the right hand over the heart.
12. Soldier in uniform, armed with rifle.
13. Sentinel on post, armed with rifle.

*An American GI, wounded in Vietnam's central
highlands, bites on stick to stifle his cries of pain.*

—UPI Photo

37. Proclaim that Mao Tse-tung is the Living God.
38. Proclaim that *you* are the Living God.
39. Stamp your foot in the earth like Rumpelstiltskin and refuse to eat until our boys return from Viet Nam.
40. Get elected Pope.
41. Get elected to the Supreme Soviet.
42. Get lost.
43. Shoot A for one month.
44. Grow seven toes on your head.
45. Commit an unnatural act with Walter Jenkins.
46. Make the world go away.
47. Wear pants made of jello.
48. Say you are a wounded veteran of the *lutte des classes.*
49. Solder your eyelids shut.

50. Ride naked through the streets on a white horse.
51. Declare war on Germany.
52. Tell the draft board that you will send your mother to fight in Viet Nam in your place.
53. Study Selective Service reports on malingering and military medicine, and/or military psychiatry texts or journal articles on the same subject, and use the clever methods they describe.
54. Organize your own army and advance on Washington.
55. Tell the psychiatrist that if he doesn't let you into the Army you'll kill him.
56. Turn yellow.
57. Infiltrate your local board.
58. Don't agree to anything.
59. Contract Addison's disease.
60. Contract Parkinson's disease.
61. Contract Bright's disease.
62. Contract Hodgkin's disease.

The Nineteenth Lesson.

THE FIRST OF MAY.

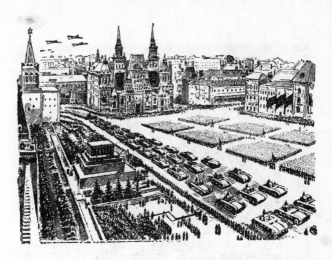

It is a warm spring morning — the morning of the First of May. Banners are **flying** over the Red Square in Moscow. Comrade Stalin, the leader and teacher of the workers of the world, is standing on the **tribune.**

The bands are playing **joyfully.** The **military parade** begins. The square is covered with tanks and **guns** and soldiers. **Silver airplanes** are flying in the sky.

The parade is over, and the demonstration begins. Comrade Stalin **raises** his hand to greet the columns of happy Soviet citizens. "Long Live the First of May!" **is written** in golden letters on the banners. And over the columns of workers we can see the portraits of Marx and Engels, Lenin and Stalin.

How happy people are to march to the tribune, singing merry songs and greeting their **beloved** leader!

(After E. Ilyin a.)

The Human Flag—A wonderful triumph of artistic military formation and photography, showing 10,000 Jackies at Great Lakes, Illinois, the largest naval training station in the world with nearly 50,000 sailors in the making, and a naval band of over 1,000 pieces. (*Copyright, U. & U.*)

63. Contract Cushing's disease.
64. Contract Fröhlich's syndrome.
65. Announce that you have become the bridegroom of the Virgin Mary.
66. Announce that you have become the bridegroom of Jesus Christ.
67. Get your friends to crucify you.
68. Counterfeit money and omit the motto *In God We Trust*.
69. Become a publisher of smut and filth.
70. Become the publisher of the Little Mao Tse-tung Library.
71. Prove that Brezhnev is a Trotskyite wrecker.
72. Burn down the building located at 39 Whitehall Street.
73. . . . 450 Golden Gate Ave.
74. . . . 536 South Clark Street.
75. . . . 55 Tremont Street.
76. . . . 916 G Street NW.
77. Burn down the Pentagon.
78. Burn baby burn.
79. Write a best-selling novel which portrays the CIA as incompetent.
80. Catch St. Anthony's fire.
81. Say you'd be happy to serve because it'll be easier to kill the fucken Americans who are interfering with the freedom of Viet Nam.
82. Recite the Pledge of Allegiance 2400 times a day.
83. Cut off your ears. In ancient times no animal was sacrificed unless it was a perfect specimen.
84. Cut off your left ear and send it to the draft board.

One man shook his head and said, "I was in Korea. If it was good enough for me and my buddies, you can go, too."

85. Grow a tail.
86. Learn to talk with your anus.
87. Become a graduate student in a subject vital to the national security, such as the epistemology of phenomenological methodology. Achieve your degree only after fifteen years of 2-S.
88. Grow old fast, or
89. When you reach the age of 17 don't get any older.
90. Drink an elixir that will cause you to shrink to a height of 2 feet 3 inches.
91. Buy a slave and send him in your place.
92. Take your girlfriend with you when you get called and insist that you will not serve unless you can sleep with her at night.
93. Take your boyfriend with you when you get called and insist that you will not serve unless you can sleep with him at night.
94. Take your mother with you when you get called and insist you will not serve unless you can sleep with *her* at night.

95. Take your chihuahua with you when you get called and insist you will not serve unless you can sleep with *it* at night.
96. Wet your bed.
97. When the doctor tells you to spread your cheeks, let him see the firecracker you have planted there beforehand.
98. Handcuff yourself to Lenin's tomb.

8 Fathers Charged With Buying Immunity From Draft for Sons

By DAVID ANDERSON

Eight fathers have been charged with trying to buy immunity from military service for their sons. Seven of the fathers were arrested in the metropolitan area yesterday, along with the young men who allegedly expected to benefit.

The arrests were made in a series of raids by agents of the Federal Bureau of Investigation. They brought to 38 the number of men named since Feb. 18 in a draft evasion conspiracy.

Thirty-one of the suspects were arraigned before Judge Leo F. Rayfiel in Federal Court, Brooklyn, yesterday. They pleaded not guilty and were released on parole to await trial.

One of the suspects is in Europe and the rest will plead later.

When Steven Barry Knobel, a husky, pink-cheeked, curly haired 22-year-old stood before the bench, United States Attorney Joseph P. Hoey told the court:

"This is the first one, typical of the entire situation. They paid a fee ranging from $1,500 to more than $5,000, depending on what the traffic would bear, to have a forged DD-44 form mailed to their local draft boards, indicating the subjects were serving satisfactorily in the armed forces reserves. They were then reclassified from 1A to 1D, exempting them from the draft."

The conspiracy was made public on Feb. 18 after the arrest of Solomon Gottfried, 56, an employe of the Nassau County Civil Service Commission, and Paul Miller, 28, a student of 98-32 57th Avenue, Elmhurst.

Mr. Gottfried supplied the

Continued on Page 8, Column 3

"We like 'em young,"
says an Army major in Vietnam.
"The young ones
take more chances."

99. Handcuff yourself to Nicholas Katzenbach and shout: "We shall not be moved!"
100. Travel to Havana.
101. Grow a long straggly black beard with maggots crawling all over it.
102. Travel to Hanoi.
103. Travel to Pyongyang.
104. Travel to Peking.
105. Travel to Washington and tell them you intend to travel to one or more of the above.
106. Publish a satirical pamphlet purporting to advise young men how to beat the draft.
107. Tell the psychiatrist that you are a closet queen.
108. Tell the security officer that you are a brother of Allen Ginsberg.
109. Tell the security officer that you are a brother of Ralph Ginzburg.
110. Hand out copies of this book at the induction center. When they tell you you cannot do this, ask if it's all right if you sell them.
111. Make sure that by one method or another you get to see the psychiatrist. Do not let them rush you through without your chance. If necessary you should faint, scream, or start crying.

112. Give the psychiatrist your standard three-minute lecture in favor of bisexuality, being sure to mention again and again that animals do it.

113. Tell them that you will leap into your grave laughing.

114. Run for the House of Representatives on the platform that Red China should be invited to send its surplus population to colonize New York and Arizona.

115. Commence psychotherapy with Dr. Robert Soblen.

116. Ask Gus Hall to go down to the induction center for you the day you are called.

117. Write a letter to the New York *Daily News* stating that the Viet Cong are nothing more than peace-loving agrarian reformers.

118. Use an American flag for a breechclout.

119. Contract tertiary syphilis.

120. Steal a laser and fight it out with the CIA.

121. Develop bleeding stigmata.

122. Cop out.

123. Conspire with a known homosexual in the Soviet embassy in Ankara.

124. Conspire with a known heterosexual in the U.S. embassy in Ankara.

125. Become chairman of the Committee to Legalize Marijuana.

126. Develop an otherworldly metaphysical system and live by its precepts.

127. Cut off your head.

128. Cut off your sergeant's head. (NAPA)*

---

* Not a pacifist act.

129. Walk into the induction center carrying an octopus.

130. Burn your draft card over CBS Television.
131. Write to Bill Buckley that you want to possess him, body and soul.
132. Set up an illegal television station on a ship outside the three-mile limit, and telecast a demand for the impeachment of Pres. Johnson. Dress up the presentation with movies showing Johnson and foreign women ambassadors engaged in sexual congress with one another.
133. Tell the psychiatrist that FBI men are looking for secret messages in your feces.
134. Wear a large brassiere around your waist.
135. Offer the psychiatrist $2.00 if he will allow you to perform an unnatural act on his person.
136. Hire an airplane to drop 100,000 of Corliss Lamont's leaflets over Danang Air Base.
137. Exercise your vereter until it becomes three feet long.
138. Marry Bettina Aptheker.
139. Join the Mau Mau.
140. Kidnap Charles Lindbergh's son.
141. Kidnap Douglas MacArthur's son.
142. Kidnap Dwight D. Eisenhower's son.
143. Kidnap John Eisenhower's son.
144. Kidnap Lyndon Johnson's son.
145. Tie your foreskin to your nose.
146. Refuse to sign the loyalty oath and when asked why say you don't feel loyal to a government of murderers.
147. Cripple your 79-year-old mother and kill your brothers and sisters and then be the sole support of your crippled 79-year-old mother.
148. Eat hair pie.
149. Bite the psychiatrist.

150. Get put in jail till you're over the draft age.
151. Don't enlist.
152. Tell the psychiatrist to spread his cheeks because you suspect him of hiding marijuana there.
153. Bring a note from Cardinal Spellman saying that you're excused.

LBJ's 'No Truth' Tag Accurate

(Associated Press Radiofoto)

Henry Cabot Lodge talks with newsmen in Saigon yesterday.

Washington, March 16 (AP)—President Johnson told a news conference last week there was "no truth" to reports that he was looking for a successor to Henry Cabot Lodge as ambassador to South Vietnam. White House Press Secretary George Christian was asked about this today. He said Johnson's statement March 9 was absolutely accurate—that the President had already picked Ambassador at Large Ellsworth Bunker to succeed Lodge.

Johnson made the announcement yesterday in a speech at Nashville, Tenn.

154. Shoot up the walls of the room, screaming: "I am the last Stalinist! I am the last Stalinist!"
155. Walk out of the induction center on tippy toes.
156. Don't compromise with the bourgeoisie.
157. Escape.
158. Pray for the end of conscription.
159. Ask the draft board for verification of your birth.
160. Make a run for it.
161. Become indispensable to the coffin industry.
162. Tell them you'll send your money to fight in Viet Nam if they'll let you stay home.
163. Don't give your right name.

164. Lose your draft card.
165. Lose your mind.
166. Ask to have the question repeated.
167. Laugh in their faces.
168. Act natural.
169. Decline the honor.
170. Chew tobacco with your ass and when the proctologist examines you spit it out.
171. Capitalize on your deficits.
172. Say you don't want to go to an all-boys' school.
173. When you go to the men's room, drop your papers and get a little shit on them by accident.
174. When the psychiatrist asks you if you hear voices say Yeah but you don't hear his.
175. Stop your artificial pacemaker.
176. Spit in their faces.
177. Have a bad reputation.

Sorry

about

that.

178. Do not be moved.
179. Tell them you already have a job with the Reichssicherheitshauptamt.
180. Say you have been appointed editor of *American Opinion* and you have no time to serve in the Army.

181. Tell them you are a wandering Jew and you have to get going.
182. Forget it.
183. Don't hide your dark under a bush.
184. Stand back.
185. Don't volunteer.
186. Tell them the Thirteenth Amendment outlawed involuntary servitude and you're not going to violate the Constitution of the United States.
187. Join the Disabled Veterans of America.
188. Refuse to testify against yourself.
189. Be bad.
190. Break a leg.
191. Be a high-born lady.
192. Join the NSU (Non-Specific Urethritis).
193. Order William F. Buckley to serve in your place.
194. Give away copies of the *Communist Manifesto* to the other inductees.
195. Go to another part of the woods.

> "Was listening to the radio to-
> night and learned that all kinds of
> demonstrations and protests are
> going on against what we are here
> for. I know one thing: those sorry
> .... doing the protesting are
> Communist or Communist in-
> spired. I don't want anyone to ever
> question or remark about U.S.
> forces being here . . . I just couldn't
> take it with what we are going
> through."

196. Live in sin.
197. Fuck for peace.
198. Never register.
199. Cut off your trigger finger.
200. Cut off your trigger.
201. Cut off your pinky.
202. Cut off your third finger.
203. Cut off your fourth finger.
204. Cut off your thumb.
205. Cut off the trigger finger on your left hand.
206. Cut off the pinky on your left hand.
207. Cut off the third finger on your left hand.
208. Cut off the fourth finger on your left hand.
209. Cut off your left arm.
210. Cut off your right arm.
211. Cut off your right leg.
212. Cut off your left leg.
213. Cut off your right penis.
214. Cut off your left penis. NB: Do not cut off your head or you will be immediately accepted.
    Also, don't cut off your left thumb because you may need it to help a wounded soldier.
215. Scream for help.

216. Go to your air raid shelter and remain there for the duration.
217. Eat five pounds of beans before your rectal examination. When the doctor comes around, don't hold back.
218. Become radioactive.
219. Swallow a live hand grenade.

> The reason I will not go into the army is that I will not kill another person. Nor will I take part in the activities and support of an institution whose purpose is to provide men who will kill when someone decides it is necessary . . . Except for its unique, gruesome function of killing people, the army is only one of many institutions in the United States which contribute to making people afraid, lonely, angry, hurt, stupid and ugly. And of all institutions, the army is only the most overt, because it alone says that you can take out your anger and fear and hurt openly by killing somebody. What finally keeps me from returning to the United States and protesting the evils of Selective Service by going to jail for refusing induction is the realization that America's problems are only unique in the way they manifest themselves, but that they are actually human problems. I can work on them anywhere. For me the way to alter things is to create alternatives. Becoming a Canadian citizen is one such alternative and I have availed myself of the opportunity (to become one).

HER POEM MAKES U.S.
CANCEL AS SUBSCRIBER

The Presbyterian Board of Christian Education said today the Defense Dept. has canceled 13,000 subscriptions to its Sunday School magazine because of a poem on napalm in the February issue by a 12-year-old girl.

The Defense Dept. described the poem as "An embarrassing item concerning Vietnam," the board said.

The item is a poem describing the dropping of napalm on a village in North Vietnam. It was written by Barbara Beidler of Vero Beach, Fla.

The magazine is used in Protestant Sunday Schools of American military bases around the world and it aimed at the 9 to 12-year-old group.

The poem is titled, "Afterthoughts on Napalm Drop on Jungle Villages near Haiphong."

"Then there was the flash—
   silver and gold,
Silver and gold.
Silver birds flying.
Golden water raining.
The rice ponds blazed with
   new water.
The jungle burst into gold and
   sent up little birds of fire
Little animals with fur aflame.
Then the children flamed.
Running—their clothes flying
   like fiery kites.
Screaming—their screams
Dying as their faces seared.
The women's baskets burned on
   their heads.
The men's boats blazed on the
   rice waters.
Then the rains came.
A rag, fire black, fluttered.
A curl of smoke rose from a
   rice stem.
The forest lay singed and
   seared.
A hut crumbled.
And all was still
Listen Americans,
Listen clear and long.
The children are screaming
in the jungles of Haiphong"

　　　—(N.Y. Post, 2/15/67).

220. Write an exposé in the *National Enquirer* about the morals convictions of J. Edgar Hoover and Cardinal Ottaviani.
221. Hand an anti-war leaflet to a soldier at the Oakland Army Terminal.
222. Write to your Senator asking for special privileges.
223. Have your mother write to your Senator asking for special privileges.
224. Become a mother.
225. Roll up to the draft board in a wheelchair with a broken leg and wave your crutch, screaming: "On to Belgrade! On to Belgrade!"
226. Contract out.
227. Cover up your tracks, or

Figure 12.--Smash-Delivery.

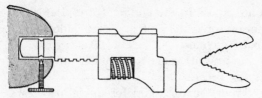

FIG. 193. – Type IX : Main de mécanicien.

228.   . . . reveal your tracks (left and right arms and legs, buttocks, penis, vagina, bellybutton, etc.).
229.   Hire a *remplaçant*.
230.   Bribe a draft official.
231.   Marry a draft official's daughter.
232.   Marry a draft official.
233.   Become obese.
234.   Gather ye rosebuds while ye may.
235.   Take the cash and let the credit go.
236.   Nor heed the rumble of a distant drum.
237.   Eat shit (this is also a way to live without working, as some of you may remember).*

---

* Half of the author is pointing with unpardonable pride to his *1001 Ways to Live Without Working*.

238.   Don't fight.
239.   Go to Copenhagen.
240.   Take benzedrine.
241.   Take dexedrine.
242.   Take methedrine.
243.   Take LSD (two cubes).
244.   Send your brother.
245.   Send in your place a poor spic who can't afford to go to college.
246.   Send in your place a poor nigger who can't afford to go to college.
247.   Or send a poor WASP even.

Utilization and Disposal Service
Real Property Division
Building 41, Denver Federal Center
Denver, Colorado 80225

February 15, 1966

Re: Invitation for Bid
     No. D-Ariz-488

NORMAN SOLOMON
P.O. BOX 190
VILLAGE STATION
NEW YORK, NEW YORK   10014

The following described property will be offered for sale by
competitive sealed bids to be opened on March 17, 1966. If you
wish to receive a copy of the Invitation for Bids, containing
bidding forms and full instructions for submitting a bid, please
return this announcement to this office.

    Yuma Air Force Station (Z-162) located twelve miles
    south of Yuma, Arizona, consisting of 20.02 acres of
    land improved with six buildings, water and sewer
    systems, and perimeter 6' chain link fence.

The property is being offered for sale as one unit on cash or
credit terms.

Harold E. Zimmer

HAROLD E. ZIMMER
Chief, Real Property Division
Utilization and Disposal Service

248. Lie down in the street and tell the cop that your left front tire blew out.

249. Don't sign any papers.

250. Resign your citizenship.

251. Tell 'em you don't hate nobody.

252. Tear up your *contrat social*.

253. Quote the Nuremberg Trial on individual responsibility, in the original German, and then shout: "Ich bin nicht Adolf Eichmann!" at the top of your lungs.

254. Set up your own country.

255. Ask forgiveness.

256. Take power.

257. Keep a dead whore in your cave.

258. Break wind as you're sworn in, thereby invalidating the whole procedure ex post farto.

259. Admit you're a spy for a foreign government (England).

260. Tell them you don't do anything just because someone tells you to.

261. Dance.

262. Laugh.

263. Die in a foreign army.

264. Don't sign your birth certificate.

265. Tell them you're innocent.

266. Ask them who they think they are.

267. Offer to love thine enemy as thyself.

268. Ask for another chance.

269. Ask for volunteers.

270. Dance naked in Times Square in support of our boys in Viet Nam.

271. Send a German shepherd instead because you heard that a German shepherd is worth ten soldiers (especially against women).

272. Kill without a uniform (i.e. murder someone in civilian life).
273. Impress a callow youth in your place.
274. Enlist simultaneously in four branches of the Service plus the Chilean Navy, and sail for the banks of the Swiss.
275. Run for President.
276. Become President.
277. Become a general.
278. Become a bear.
279. Become a snake.
280. . . . an alligator.
281. . . . an alligator pear.
282. . . . a persimmon.
283. . . . peach.
284. . . . plum.
285. . . . pit.
286. . . . seed.

287. . . . rock.
288. . . . word.
289. . . . password.
290. . . . symbol.
291. . . . an irreplaceable part of the civilian economy (i.e. rock-'n'-roll star, draft director, funeral director, etc.).

13. Main de prêtre (Type XIII, *fig.* 199 et 200). — Il y a quelque temps, un prêtre, amputé du bras droit au niveau du tiers inférieur, vint me prier de lui faire construire une main lui permettant de dire la messe.

L'étude des mouvements et des attitudes de la main

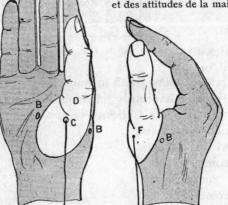

FIG. 199, 200. — Type XIII : Main de prêtre (face et profil).

A, A, Ressorts maintenant les objets saisis; D, Pouce mobile articulé sur un axe en B avec traction sur le point C; F, commande reliée au levier du coude.

gauche, pendant l'office, m'a démontré qu'elle devait remplir la fonction de préhension et de maintien d'objets dans le sens vertical, tels que le calice, et d'objets dans un plan horizontal, tels que la bourse, la patène, etc., et que, en outre, elle devait, parallèlement avec l'autre main, présenter l'attitude de la prière.

292. . . . an irreplaceable part of an automobile.

293. . . . an irreplaceable cog in the great wheels of American industry's progress.

294. . . . a Red Chinese. Since Red China doesn't exist, you can't be drafted.

295. Become a cop, or

296. Become a robber.

297. Read the *Confessions of Felix Krull* and do what he did.

298. Disguise yourself as a coward when all you really want is not to get killed.

299. Stay in your room.

300. Punch the psychiatrist in the jaw when he asks you a question, and shout: "Nobody calls *me* nuts!"

301. Ask forgiveness.

302. Ask that an enemy be brought to New York so you can strangle him to death with your bare hands over NBC-TV.

303. Write a 700-page history of buggery.

304. Demand a recount.

305. Say you're a malingerer and tell the psychiatrist malingerers don't make good soldiers.

306. Become a psychiatrist.

307. Burn your draft card.

308. Burn your draft board.

309. Burn your draft army.

310. Burn yourself up.

311. Burn the President up.

312. Burn up everybody that wants you to burn up anybody.

313. Don't wear a deodorant at the induction center.

314. Do not follow the leader.

315. Take a live chicken to bed with you every night.

316. Take a dead chicken to bed with you every night.

317. Change your sex.

GI SPUD SLICER EYES FREEDOM
Skins Out of Potato Peeling Rap

WASHINGTON, June 19 (AP).—Pfc. Andrew God Jr. now stands cleared by a court-martial of a charge that he destroyed government property.

It seems his captain and his mess sergeant felt he was peeling potatoes too thick. God, who is an Arlington, Va., architect when he's not a draftee, convinced the court-martial at Fort Myer, Va., that his potato-peeling methods were as good, if not better, than any.

THE PROSECUTION sought to show that Pfc. God had "wilfully suffered potatoes of some value, the military property of the United States, to be destroyed by improper peeling."

But God told the court-martial:

"You can't jab a potato with a knife and dig into it. If the knife slips, you've got it in your hand."

The mess sergeant, Holger M. Johnson, gave the court a demonstration of how he said God was whacking away. When Johnson got through with his demonstration potato, there wasn't much left.

But the defense counsel, Lt. Bruce Segal, proved to the court's satisfaction that the peelings sliced off by the mess sergeant weighed more than God's.

Counsel was able to show this because Capt. Thomas C. Woods, God's commanding officer, had been saving some of the God-sliced peelings for a month. He had a whole pan of them.

318. Tell them if they feel like fighting they can go right ahead but you'd just like to stay home.

319. Tell them you're not patriotic.

320. Grow another penis.

321. Tell the draft board the draft is involuntary and you don't approve of things that are involuntary.

322. Make a mess.

323. Pass a new Selective Service Act in which only men over 80 are eligible.

324. Wear spiked heels.

325. If you are not for yourself, who will be for you? If you are only for yourself, what are you? If not now, when?

326. Give in to that impulse.

327. Be alive in Argentina.

328. Rent a robot and let him be inducted in your place.

329. Challenge Richard Nixon to a debate on the proposition: "Resolved—that Lolita Haze lost her virginity before her pubic hair appeared."

330. Ask them to prove it.

331. Make sure that your files get lost at the draft board. Use several spelling variants of your name, get your sister to work at the draft board, distract the file clerk by goosing him, etc.
332. Pray that God becomes a pacifist.
333. Run to Venezuela.
334. Demand to see their credentials.
335. Go crazy.
336. Shout: "Ich bin nicht hier gekommen Ordnung zu machen!" and stamp out of the room.
337. Say you've fought already.
338. Say you're scaired.
339. Say: "Men ken dorten geharget veren!" and leave.
340. Ask what's in it for you.
341. Contradict them.
342. Raise your hand and leave the room.
343. Argue.
344. Shit with fright all over the induction center.
345. Give up (to the enemy).
346. Shout: "The enemy is at home! The enemy is at home!" (Then go home.)

347. Come to the induction center dressed all in black and when you undress have your body painted black and when asked why say: "in mourning for all future murderers and murderees.

348. Have your body painted red, white and blue.

349. Demand to see the Commander-in-Chief and then when you see the Commander-in-Chief ask him: "How's your asshole?"

350. Say you're from Berkeley.

> **Pfc Kenneth Little, cook, Geln-hausen:** Guys who get practical jokes pulled on them are usually the duds. Maybe a guy who won't take a shower. When he falls asleep, they put shaving cream in his palm about seven inches high and then they tickle his nose. When he tries to scratch it, what a mess. Then he has to clean up. Once some guy had shaving cream put all over his wall locker and clothes. They used about 12 cans and it looked like an old slapstick comedy scene. It was just before an inspection and after the first shirt walked in there were a few Article 15s passed out.

351. Say you're a member of SDS.
352. . . . SPU.
353. . . . WRL.
354. . . . PLM.
355. . . . M2M.
356. . . . FFFF.

> **Pfc Jerry Travis, cook, Geln-hausen:** There's a good one I pulled on my buddy one time. We went out and got drunk together and during the whole evening I kept telling him how I was going to tie his shoe-strings together. We kept laughing about it and finally went back to the billets and he flaked out with his clothes on. The next morning he fell flat on his face just like I promised. Now he pulls the same thing on me. No one gets mad, it's just clean fun. Helps pass the time away. I know some others, but they're too dirty to print.

> **Pfc Willie Walker, medic, Hoechst:** I've played a few, like fixing the legs on a guy's bunk so that when he gets in it folds up on him. Another good one is to tell a guy that he's got mail and that the mail clerk wouldn't give it to you. The guy goes hopping down there for nothing. Makes him madder than hell. Or shake him up by telling him you saw his name on the KP roster.

357. Ask who's in charge here and when brought before the proper officer look him up and down and say (mincingly): "Oh—are you in charge, dearie?"

358. Sell your passport in Geneva.

359. . . . Paris, France.

360. . . . Rome.

361. . . . Milan.

362. . . . Athens.

363. . . . Moscow. (Do not sell your passport in Madrid as you will not get enough for it.)

364. Smoke dried shit and offer the recruiting sergeant a cigarette, asking him if he has ever smoked "funny cigarettes" (pot) before.

> **Sp4 Buddy Parker, medic, Hoechst:** Here's a good one. Nail a guy's shower shoes to the floor. He gets up in the morning, slips into them and falls flat on his face. Guys do this sort of thing to keep up with the trend in "troop harassment." I've heard of guys having their whole bunk carried outside, but that's going too far. Why do they do it? These jokes help make things go easier, break the routine.

365. Cringe and crawl, licking the boots of the nearest officer.
366. Circulate a petition against American policy in Viet Nam at the induction center.
367. Say it's not your war.
368. Become an air raid warden.
369. Become an air raid sign.
370. Become an air raid.
371. Bomb Dresden.
372. Get dropped on Dresden.
373. Desecrate Churchill's body in Piccadilly Circus.

Pvt Robert Jones, rifleman, Kirch-Goens: Some guys buy whistles and go around blowing them in the billets making people think it's a formation. I've even had shaving cream sprayed behind my ears and in my hand, just for a joke. Then I pulled it on someone else. But just among friends. It could cause trouble by trying it with someone you don't like.

S Sgt William Curtis, illustrator, Hahn: Shaving cream seems to be the bit. Put it in a guy's boots. I've also seen whole wall lockers come down on a guy when he goes to open it. These younger GIs come up with some good ones. It's usually the same ones pulling it all the time. They get their enjoyment that way. But it gets old after awhile. Just when one guy gets tired of pulling these stunts, some new one will come along and start in. Once I had French civilians working under me and they were famous for setting a pail of water in a man's wall locker, propped up somehow so that when the poor guy opened it, he just couldn't help getting drenched.

374. Write a 9000-page treatise on farts and their relation to character.
375. Convert to pacifism.
376. Convert to Christianity.
377. Pass 'em by.
378. Challenge the challengers.
379. Go your own way.
380. Say: I gave already.

The frauds resorted to by enrolled and drafted men to escape service are, in our experience, very numerous. Every species of falsehood and misrepresentation is indulged in to feign disease where none exists. Rheumatism, "weak back," "stitch in the side," hemorrhoids, lameness from old fractures, old sprains, loss of sight of one or both eyes, disease of the heart, consumption, hæmorrhage from the lungs, disease of the kidneys, ankylosed joints, and deafness, do not comprise even the tithe of diseases feigned by those who wish to escape service. The loss of sight of the right eye is claimed very often without cause. During the first draft, conscripts frequently came with the pupil so dilated that the eye presented the appearance of organic change. After exempting several who came first with this disability, I suspected fraud. We arrested two from one sub-district, and had them properly brought before the board. They paid commutation and were dismissed. Within both to be sound, and held both to service. I re-examined them, found the eyes of one year afterward, one of these men enlisted for a bounty, and entered the service with a pair of sound eyes. I had reason often afterward to suspect the application of belladonna to the eye.

Under these circumstances, we examined the pockets of the man, and placed him rigidly under guard until the nature of the case was clearly revealed. Irritating substances, such as sand or dirt, are sometimes thrown into the eyes by conscripts for the purpose of producing conjunctivitis preparatory to examination. When a man claims exemption from total loss of sight of right eye, if I can see no evidence of disease, before I decide his case, I close the left eye perfectly, quietly stand a little to one side, and order him, in a peremptory manner and sharp tone, to "Look at me;" if the sight is totally gone, the right eye is motionless, but if any sight remains, before he is aware, the eye involuntarily turns with its axis toward me, which satisfies me that he is attempting deception. I will here state that I have never used the ophthalmoscope to explore the eye.

Men frequently purge themselves preparatory to examination with aloes and other drastic articles to bring on hæmorrhoids. These cases are generally detected by an erythematous discoloration of the skin, radiating from the anus to the distance of one, two, or three inches, connected with alternate contraction and relaxation of the sphincter ani. A great many men, otherwise sound, have had all the teeth extracted from the upper jaw. A considerable proportion of these, I have no doubt, resorted to extraction to avoid service. Some came with gums lacerated and swollen from having had the teeth removed within a few days of examination, while others had their teeth removed perhaps several months previous. When we had reason to suspect that drafted men had their teeth extracted to defraud the Government, we held them to service if they were otherwise sound, and assigned reasons for so doing, which were sent with them to the rendezvous.

Drafted men frequently came with one or more fingers or a great toe cut squarely off, the bone protruding, making a very sore stump, which they represented as the result of recent accident. They were also held to service, and reasons sent forward why they were held.

SURGEONS' REPORTS—WISCONSIN—FIFTH DISTRICT.

The scrotum was evidently inflamed, tender, and much thickened, feeling much like a large, solid, corrugated orange. The cellular tissue was so thickened, extending above the pubes, that it was quite impossible satisfactorily to inspect the inguinal region, or to come to any definite conclusion as to the cause of the difficulty. On a more careful inspection, however, I discovered a fine crepitus, as of air in the cellular tissue about the pubes, and, in one instance, *in the prepuce*; this led me to suspect a trick, and on pushing my investigations I learned that an incision had been made in one or more places in the scrotum, a blow-pipe inserted, and the surrounding parts completely filled with air. The orifice was then closed, and healed, the air remaining *in situ*, and apparently producing inflammation of the parts. I subsequently learned that this deception was not uncommon among Bohemians in Europe.

GEN. GEORGE E. STRATEMEYER, HERO OF THE KOREAN WAR URGES READING OF THE IRON CURTAIN OVER AMERICA

GENERAL GEORGE E. STRATEMEYER

THE IRON CURTAIN OVER AMERICA is the sensational book written by Colonel John Beaty, formerly top man in Military Intelligence during World War II. In this book he reveals that Jews and their descendants who have migrated to the United States have seized control of our political parties and many of our cultural and educational organizations—even churches. It is the most courageous book ever written by a contemporary intellectual on the subject of the Jew.

Colonel Beaty is head of the English Department in America's largest Methodist University, known as Southern Methodist University of Dallas, Texas. Every mature, intelligent citizen, including professors, clergymen, enlightened private citizens and public officials should have this book. It contains 268 pages. It documents itself. It is beautifully bound in cloth. The price is $3.00.

Address all orders to Christian Nationalist Crusade, P. O. Box 27895, Los Angeles 27, California.

381. Give a chocolate kiss instead.
382. Kiss the army people instead. A big fat kiss on the mouth.
383. Ask for an explanation.
384. Say: No, thank you.

Moment of death ... A Marine throws up his rifle as a Viet Cong bullet hits him. His body will be collected and flown back to his base packed in a plastic bag

SANDY PICKREL—"I think we are approaching the time when we will have to draft women. Women are coming up in the world."

National Headquarters
SELECTIVE SERVICE SYSTEM
Washington, D. C.

November 13, 1940

FOR IMMEDIATE RELEASE   Release No. 110

From the Mexican State of Coahuila which borders on the American State of Texas comes a story of the patriotism of an American-born citizen of Mexican extraction who registered for Selective Service in the United States, returned to his home where he was fatally wounded and then made the dying request that his picture be taken in his coffin so that no one would believe he was hiding to escape training under the American Selective Service Law.

The story was revealed today by the State Department when making public correspondence from G. R. Willson, American Consul, Piedras Negras, Coahuila, Mexico, who wrote concerning the attitude of American-born men of Mexican ancestry who registered in the United States for Selective Service and who went back to their Mexican homes until such time as they might be called for training by local boards of the United States.

One of these registrants was Tomas Godina who, on October 16, crossed the border to register for service as an American citizen. Just eleven days later he was mortally wounded in a fight in Mexico.

On his deathbed he told his mother and sister with whom he lived:

"After I am dead have my picture taken in my coffin so that if I am called to service in the United States and do not come you can show the picture and everyone will know I am not hiding somewhere trying to avoid service in the American Army."

The correspondence was forwarded from the State Department to C. A. Dykstra, director of Selective Service.

385. Stand outside Army Intelligence headquarters on E. 16th Street and take pictures of every person who enters. When questioned, say that you are gathering material for a series on war criminals.

386. Ask for a presidential pardon.

387. Become a baby.

388. Say: "My mother won't let me."

389. Stay stuck in your girlfriend's vagina. Army too embarrassed to take you out.

390. Ask the judge to go in your place; you stay in his place.

391. Say you don't have shoes and point to your bare feet.

392. Eat your toe jam in front of the psychiatrist without offering him any.

393. Carry your artificial vagina in convenient tuck-away container with you to induction center. Offer to demonstrate it to examining urologist.

394. Take Enovid.

395. Tell them you like Theatre of the Absurd but this is too much.

396. Be a Jewish mother, or

397. Be a Jewish mother's son, or

398. Be a Jewish schizophrene.

399. Lie.

400. Lie better than them.

401. Demand to see the man responsible for the war.

402. Admit you are Jack the Ripper but refuse appointment except as a captain.

403. Tell them the smell of burning flesh makes you vomit and you'd dirty the sergeant's uniform.

404. Ask: "Exactly what are the advantages of being in the Army?"

405. Admit you really are not a citizen.

406. Ask who's going to pay for repairs to the uniform.

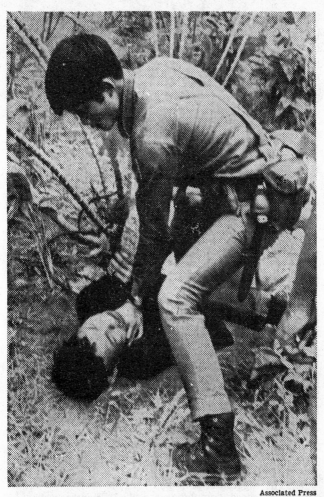

Associated Press

INTERROGATION: A South Vietnamese soldier using force to question a Vietcong suspect at Ngoc recently.

407. Say: "Millions for defense and $500 if you get me out of here."

408. Say you're a lover, not a fighter.

409. Say: "I'd rather be fucked than President."

410. Ask if this can't all be settled by Games Strategy.

411. Say: "Thanks, but I've already had a war."

412. Say you were killed in the last war.

413. Tell them to show movies of the last war and then everyone can stay in their parlors.

414. Drop LSD in the Peking reservoir.

415. Drop LSD in the Hanoi reservoir.

416. Drop LSD in the Potomac.

417. Tell them that two wrongs don't make a right.

418. Say you're not really dependable.

419. Demand a trial by your peers: other inductees; then release each other.

420. Say you're a dreamer.

WASHINGTON, Feb. 8 (UPI)—Rep. Frank Thompson Jr., D-N.J., is not asking what their country can do for the Daughters of the American Revolution. He is suggesting what the Daughters of the American Revolution can do for their country.

Thompson, not one to shrink from his duty when national security is involved, has volunteered the patriotic women's group for a special mission in Viet Nam. He made the move in a reply to a speech by Rep. Craig Hosmer, R-Calif.

Hosmer suggested that since the Vietnamese were known to be superstitious about things as seeing a woman at dawn, the United States might profit by dropping plastic models of women, among other things, on early morning raids against North Viet Nam.

"The suggestion of dropping plastic women in dawn raids is indeed stimulating," replied Thompson, "but . . . compromised by Mr. Hosmer's disturbing addiction to the synthetic.

"Why should we be content with polystyrene when the Daughters of the American Revolution are clamoring to do their bit?"

421. Tell Hershey that he should draft only convicted forgers.
422. Tell Hershey that he should draft only convicted perjurers.
423. Tell Hershey that he should draft only convicted rapists.
424. Tell Hershey that he should draft only convicted sodomites.
425. Tell Hershey to fuck himself.
426. Draw the line.

FEZ, Morocco, March 3 — King Hassan II announced today the institution of compulsory military service in a speech on the 10th anniversary of Moroccan independence and the 5th anniversary of his accession to the throne.

AWOL Soldier Seized

WILKES-BARRE, Pa., March 18 (UPI)—James Richmond, 20-year-old serviceman who had been absent without leave from the Army since last June, was picked up by the Federal Bureau of Investigation Friday as he hid in a tunnel in the cellar of his mother's home in nearby Hanover Township.

Many Draftees Decline To Fight the Strike

Since the city's transit strike began, about one-third of the 175 men ordered to report daily for induction into the Armed Services have apparently decided they were not essential and have stayed home.

Col. Paul Akst, director of the city's Selective Service System, said last night that of the 500 to 600 men expected each day for pre-induction physical examinations, only about one-third had reported.

The induction dates for the tardy men, he said, would be set forward and they would not be penalized.

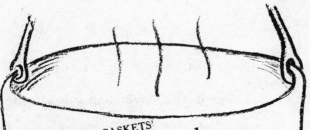

'FLAG-DRAPED CASKETS'

Youth, 20, Arrested After Draft Protest

A 20-year-old Big Lake youth was being held in Hennepin County Jail under $10,000 bond today on a charge that he dumped two buckets of human exerement into the files of the Sherburne County draft board at Elk River.

Held is Barry Bondhus, who was arrested by FBI agents Thursday night at his home.

He is one of 12 children of Thomas Bondhus, 43, who operates machine shops at Big Lake, Monticello and Orrock in Sherburne County.

Sidney Abramson, assistant U.S. district attorney, said the youth would be given a hearing today before U.S. Commissioner Bernard Zimpfer in Minneapolis Federal Court.

THE MINNEAPOLIS STAR
Fri., Feb. 25, 1966 ★

The arrest of the youth apparently climaxed a series of difficulties he and his father have had with the draft board.

The elder Bondhus said he has told the board repeatedly that he is opposed to any of his sons serving in the armed forces.

"If you draft Barry I have nothing to look forward to for the next 24 years but flag-draped caskets," he said.

Barry is the second oldest of 10 Bondhus boys.

After a board hearing Feb. 15, the youth was classified 1-A and ordered to take a pre-induction physical examination in Minneapolis.

The FBI said the youth refused to co-operate.

Wednesday, the complaint charged, young Bondhus walked into the board's office and dumped the substance into six draft board file cases. His draft board status still is pending.

After Bondhus shit-in, the draft board moved from the Elk River American Legion building, where it formerly was housed, to a new office in the First National Bank. Professional fumigators have been brought in from Minneapolis to air out the old office, but it is still not in use.

Ballad of the SS Troop

Soldiers fighting in the East.
Fearless men against the Slavic beast.
Men who fight for Farben and Krupp.
The brave men of the SS Troop.

> Double S upon their chest.
> These are men--the Führer's best.
> One hundred men try to join the group,
> But only three make the SS Troop.

Trained to live for the Führer's goals.
Trained in dealing with Jews and Poles.
Men who fight like Jürgen Stroop
Courage take from the SS Troop.

> Double S upon their chest.
> These are men--the Führer's best.
> One hundred men try to join the group,
> But only three make the SS Troop.

Back at home a Hausfrau waits.
Her SS-man has met his fate.
He has died in Deutschland's quest
Leaving her his last request:

> "Put the double S on my son's chest.
> Make him one of the Führer's best.
> He'll be the man for an Einsatz group.
> Have him join the SS Troop."

427. Tell them God is on your side; if they say God is on their side, answer OK, it's a draw, let's go home.
428. Demand to see the injured party.
429. Go limp.
430. Tell them your mother was a Viet Cong.
431. Resist bodily.
432. Say no.
433. Say you are already in the army of the unemployed.
434. . . . the ignorant.
435. . . . the dying.
436. . . . the unhappy.
437. Tell them that you think the war is illegal and that you *never* break the law.

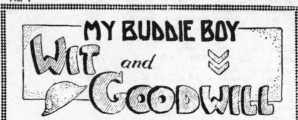

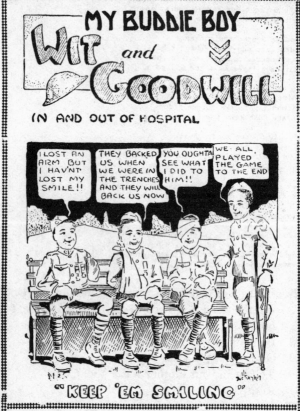

A Smile for the winner.   A Tear for the dying.

A Dollar for the Needy

Read! Laugh! Cry! Be good to the Soldiers!

To be sold by Ex-Service Men only as a means of self-support

Price 25 Cents

438. Bomb Hanoi with platinum ingots.
439. Bomb Hanoi with uncircumcised catamites.
440. Bomb Hanoi with puppy-dogs' tails.
441. Bomb Hanoi with snail shells that still smell of garlic.
442. Bomb Hanoi with old copies of *The New York Times.*
443. Bomb Hanoi with 42nd Street hustlers.
444. Bomb Hanoi with registered nurses.
445. Bomb Hanoi with garlands of peonies.
446. Bomb Hanoi with goose down.
447. Bomb Hanoi with Allen Ginsberg.
448. Bomb Hanoi with O-bombs (orgasm bombs).
449. Bomb Hanoi with parakeets.
450. Bomb Hanoi with Hallmark greeting cards.

Figure 18.--Jab to the Midsection.

451. Bomb Hanoi with Bibles, R. S. V.
452. Bomb Hanoi with Mme. de Gaulle.
453. Bomb Hanoi with the finest quality marijuana.
454. Bomb Hanoi with Christian Science leaflets.
455. Bomb Hanoi with Jewish Science leaflets.
456. Ask for a cup to put your stools in, then ask for a spoon.
457. Back out.
458. Be a (necessarily deferred) civil statistician for the U.S. Armed Forces casualty counters. Be civil, don't upset mothers. (Remember, figures don't lie but liars figure.)
459. Demand to be treated according to the Geneva Convention for prisoners of war.
460. Get a WAC with child. We don't want Welfare supporting our fatherless children. Added benefit: she gets out too. Live happily ever after.
461. Say:· I do not choose to fight.
462. Show them your peace button.
463. Explain to them that having your guts bayoneted out makes you sick to your stomach.

Could Win in a Flash, U.S. Air Chief Says

464. Tell them that you are a man *already*.
465. Laugh in their faces.
466. Question their motives.
467. Commit lust.
468. Recite:

> I strive with none
> For none are worth my strife.

469. Carry a sign that says FUCK THE DRAFT.
470. Carry a sign that says FUCK FOR PEACE.
471. Go to jail, or
472. Get married.
473. Get married twice, or
474. Go to jail twice.
475. Get married three times then go immediately to a psychiatrist.
476. Dismount and run for it.
477. Ask to be reclassified as a protected species.
478. Disappear.
479. Contemplate the horror of murder.
480. Sleep late with your warm girlfriend.
481. Tell them you'll think about it.
482. Go home.

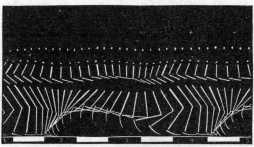

FIG. 7.—Positions of the Extremities of the Soldier During "Double Time." Photographs taken at the rate of sixty per second. (After Marey.)

483. Decide once and for all not to go.

484. Nod out.

485. Shout: "I don't take no shit from no one!"

486. Walk up to the colonel and his lady and with a big grin on your face pinch her double chin and ask her if she and Judy O'Grady are really the same under the skin.

487. Say: "Let a machine do it."

488. Throw a fit.

489. Conquer your fear of being a coward.

490. Ask for your life back.

491. Get a letter of reference from the authors of this book.

492. Deny you are guilty and ask why you are being sentenced to death.

493. Giggle.

494. Masturbate with one hand.

495. Have MAKE LOVE NOT WAR painted on the front of your underpants.

496. Have an essential civilian job like liar for the U.S. State Department.

497. Shoot a water pistol at the sergeant and say: Bang! you're dead!

498. Say you are afraid of crab lice, or

499. Say Good! now I can get to eat all the crab lice I want.

500. Keep singing at the top of your lungs even though the colonel orders you to stop.

Drawn by Robert Minor, July 1916

ARMY MEDICAL EXAMINER: "At last a perfect soldier!"

501. Use legerdemain.
502. Bring the general up on charges.
503. Ask which way they went (then go the other way).
504. Make a citizen's arrest of the President.
505. Tell them you have just begun to fight—the draft board.
506. Practice shooting on the induction line.
507. Prove that you are Christ.
508. Free all prisoners.
509. Cry:

> Charity charity!
> Come out of charity
> And peace with me in America.

510. Tell them to start all over.
511. Start all over.
512. Let the kids out of the schools.
513. Be a pagan suckled in a creed outworn.
514. Go gay.

Detroit, Mich.: William Bunge, a geography professor at Wayne State issued the following statement concerning his protest of the war: ". . .I will not become a finger man for the Selective Service. I will not give a grade lower than C to any young man, even if he supports the war. Today's announcement that college students are about to lose their deferment merely means that I will escalate my grades in step with their escalation of the drafting of students to be butchered thousands of miles away. I will not fail any one of my students merely for below C work. It is not a just punishment. D stands for Death."

> If Colonel Bell demanded a lot from his men, he showed that he was willing to give them the best. Visitors say that his messhall serves the best food in Vietnam. Furthermore, Ding Dong has eliminated K.P.
>
> "Pot walloping is below the dignity of a rifleman," he says. "What I did was to contract to sell my garbage for $77 a month for pig food. With that money I hire Vietnamese to do the cleaning up."

515. Sneak out.

516. Become an atheist because "there are no atheists in foxholes."

517. Demand that all patriotic readers of the New York *Daily News* be drafted immediately and sent to the front (especially the ones who write the letters to the editor).

518. Write a 3000-page treatise which proves that drinking vaginal secretions from the source prevents cancer.

519. Write to the War Resisters League, 6 Beekman Street, New York, N.Y. 10038.

520. Write to the Central Committee for Conscientious Objectors, 2006 Walnut Street, Philadelphia 3, Pa.

521. Consult your local Students for a Democratic Society chapter (this is an unsolicited and probably unwanted commercial).

522. Consult your local Student Peace Union chapter.

523. Go to your synagogue and pray you find a rabbi who will testify in your behalf.

524. Go to your church and pray you find a priest or minister who will testify in your behalf.

525. Go to your mosque and pray you find an imam who will testify in your behalf.

526. Ask to see their papers.

Russian pacifists oppose war

COLONEL GAGARIN, the Russian astronaut, in a speech which was later broadcast, recently attacked young Russian pacifists who, he said, believed there was no need for an army, and that there would be no war.

"These demagogues cannot grasp that fighting is not just a possibility; it is going on now, with weapons in hand. Vietnam is an example", he said.

The admission that there is pacifist agitation in Russia, of such a nature as to demand condemnation by so influential a figure as Yuri Gagarin, is most remarkable.

527. Ask to see their papers and when they show you their papers rip them up.

528. Don't tell them anything but your name, your class rank and your IBM number.

529. Yell: "Help!"

530. Tell them you believe in loving your enemy.

531. Send a telegram to Pres. Johnson suggesting that he volunteer as a private in the infantry to help the war effort.

532. Walk into the induction center with a voodoo doll that looks like Gen. Hershey. Stick pins into it and yell: "That'll fix the bastard for picking on me!" If Hershey dies, say it was all a joke and you're not superstitious anyway.

533. Board a Staten Island ferry and point a real toy gun at the pilot and force him to sail to Havana. If you are caught, explain that you wanted to show the passengers how bad Castro's Cuba is.

534. Lick your latrine clean.

535. Try to smuggle in 100 kilos of pure heroin from Marseilles. If you're caught you'll be exempt from the draft as a convicted felon. If you get away with it you'll be so rich that you can bribe Gen. Hershey, or even Pres. Johnson.

536. Smoke grass, or if that doesn't work,

537. Smoke pot.

538. Smoke Mexican pot.

539. Smoke ... more ... zz ... Mexican pot ... zzz ...

540. ... zzz ... some ... pot ... more ... zzz ...

541. ... pot ... some ... more ... smoke ... zzzzz ...

542. ... zzz ... pot ... zzz ...

543. ... zzzzzz ...

544. Reveal your secret self.

545. Manufacture sanitary napkins decorated with portraits of Mme. Nhu and Mme. Chiang.

Associated Press Wirephoto
Jeering crowd of angry youths, many of them high school students on their way to school, attacks draft card burners on steps of Boston courthouse. John A. Phillips, 22 (center, light coat) was beaten so severely he was hospitalized.

546. Hire a cheap Jew to serve in your place.
547. Hire a servile Negro to serve in your place.
548. Hire a duplicitous Communist to serve in your place.
549. Sing "Kill for Peace" LOUD at the induction center.
550. Speak bigly but carry a soft stick.
551. Be a leper-licker.
552. Go to Juárez.
553. Go to D.F.
554. Go to Agua Caliente.
555. Do not go to Acapulco (too many draft dodgers).
556. Sacrifice one of your arms and as they pull you in your arm comes off in their hands and then you run away.
557. Threaten to call the police if they don't stop bothering you.
558. Weep hysterically.
559. Steal Gen. Eisenhower's used underpants and auction them off at Parke-Bernet and donate the proceeds to SNCC.
560. Explain to them the theory that frustration and aggression are the causes of war.
561. Don't run until you see the whites of their eyes.
562. Weep for Adonais for he will die.
563. Accuse them of operating a slaughterhouse without a license.

564. Take over the country and throw a huge block party from San Francisco to the New York islands.
565. Riot.
566. Marry a Viet Cong.
567. Since practicing psychotherapists in most states do not have to have academic degrees, band together with your friends and set up another friend as one. (This is quite simple—just rent a cheap office and order a ream of stationery. If you have ten friends the whole caper will cost less than $10 each.) Your newly-created mind expert will give each of you a letter which says that you are insane and must not be drafted.
568. Feel love toward everyone and kiss everyone you meet. The Army will think you insane and throw you out faster than you can say Fuck for Peace.
569. Accept a foreign title.
570. Vote in a foreign election.
571. Pull the rope off your neck, shouting: "I only regret that I have but one life!"
572. Bite.
573. Freeze yourself.
574. Eat ape shit with a shovel.
575. Become a flower.
576. Go down on God.
577. Ask the advice of your minister, priest, rabbi, imam, guru or shaman.

> The two girls first put forth the plan in the Wheaton News, a student newspaper. They said they got the idea from Aristophanes' "Lysistrata," a Greek play in which women give up sex in an effort to get their husbands to give up war.

578. When you report for induction, answer all questions with a single nonsense word, such as *grobble*. When they send you to the psychiatrist, vary the rhythm with:

> Grobble grobble
> Grobble grobble
> Grobble grobble grobble.

579. Deliterate yourself.

580. Commit an original sin.

581. Take a crap in your urine bottle. When they give you another one spit in it. If they give you a third jerk off in it.

582. Have a peashooter concealed in your shoes and shoot peas at the various doctors.

583. Love yourself above abstractions.

584. Start early. When you're 12 years old, enlist simultaneously in the Army and the Navy. (They'll let you out immediately when they find out you're under age.) The next year enlist again. Keep this up and you will impress the officials that you are unstable and should not be allowed in no matter how old you are.

585. Take good care of yourself. You belong to yourself.

586. Walk into the induction center carrying a big portrait of Mao Tse-tung. When asked why, say:

"Because I take my orders from *him* and I don't care what you jerks tell me."

587. Bring a box of dead rats with you. Offer to sell one to the psychiatrist cheap.

588. Defect to a country that has no UMT.

589. Report to the induction center in drag, with obviously false eyelashes and an overabundance of facial cosmetics. Wiggle your hips seductively at the sergeant and say: "Baby, I can't wait to get in! All those bea-yoo-tiful boys . . . !"

590. Become a priest.

591. Become a nun.

592. Become a nun's priest.

593. Resign from the Gook-of-the-Month Club.

594. Refuse to kill.

595. Do not do in even such little ones as these.

596. Knock up your mother.

597. Knock up your grandmother.

598. Knock up your dog's great-grandfather.

599. Walk up your own ass and disappear.

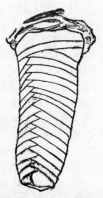

FIGURE 15. — Recurrent bandage of stump. (Wharton.)

600. Masturbate while staring at the other handsome naked young men on the line and (variant) eat your come and (subvariant) offer some to the psychiatrist.

601. Be carried in impaled on a crucifix.

602. Fart the Pledge of Allegiance.

603. Eat ten grams of radium. (Radium is very expensive but it can be recovered after you are cremated.)

604. Hide behind a typewriter.

605. Offer your wife to the induction officer.

606. Fuck Communism!

607. Tattoo the word FUCK on your penis.

608. Tattoo FUCK COMMUNISM on your forehead.

609. Ask them if you can bring your mother to camp with you.

610. Pull out your dick and ask if it's the right size to fit the girls in the country you're going to.

611. Make a bet with your induction officer that your cock is bigger than his.

612. Tell them you're a vegetarian and you will not violate your diet (no milk or eggs either).

613. Be draft-exempt.

614. Ask them if you can bugger the VC before you kill 'em.

615. Sue ten canning companies on account of "impurities" and foreign objects (feces?) found in cans of food you have bought. Tell Army officials you can't leave court cases now. Ask if Army food is pure anyway and what kind of inspection is done. Question them incessantly and be thrown out on your paranoid ass.

616. Ask if this (induction) is a good way to defect to North Viet Nam.

617. Wipe out your recruiting officer. (NAPA)

618. Show up at the induction center with a friend. Stand in line with your arms around his waist. Kiss and grope him ostentatiously. When asked why you are doing this, explain that you are expressing joy at being allowed to fight and die for your country.

619. Send Dean Rusk a bar of soap and order him to wash his mouth out every time he tells a lie.

620. Hide under the bed.

621. Go to school.

622. Go to draft-dodging school.

623. Go to grade school.

624. Go to kindergarten.

625. Suck your mommy's tittie.

626. Faint.

627. Bring your guitar and sing "Universal Soldier" without stopping.

628. Bring Buffy Sainte-Marie with you and that beautiful girl while singing "Universal Soldier."

629. Go to Times Square, find a few dozen bugger mates and get a prolapsed rectum.

630. Crawl in backwards while sucking off Allen Ginsberg.

631. Walk behind (while buggering) Allen Ginsberg chanting peace mantras.

632. Walk in dressed as a rubber fetishist.

'Suffering and privations of children do not ennoble'

Gen. William Westmoreland, sling supporting wrist he broke playing tennis, talks with Capt. Pat McCallum at Lai Khe.

633. Walk in wearing a big diaper and say: "Well, I still have some problems."

634. Take a crap in your pants and let the shit roll down to the floor.

635. Walk in with a blazing acetylene torch mumbling "Gooks gooks." If the sarge tries to take it away from you, make like to burn *him*.

636. Walk in softly with a crucifix held aloft, intoning "Pax pax pax."

637. Have your mother call up and say you're sick.

638. Bring your dog with you.

639. Bring your dog with you, having trained him to shit on the floor.

640. Bring your shitting dog with you, dress him in a heavy coat and old-fashioned cap and two pairs of pants, and mumble to anyone who will or will not listen: "So who's going to take care of Poopsie?"

641. Sell double-indemnity-for-accidental-death insurance policies to draftees while on line.

642. Throw cherry bombs at doctors while on the examination line, hollering: "The gooks! The gooks are coming! Take cover!"

643. Tell them that if they don't leave you alone you'll reveal who *really* killed Kennedy.

644. Do a book like this and during the research find other ways.

645. Study the *Handbook for Conscientious Objectors* published by the Central Committee for Conscientious Objectors.

646. Read Selective Service reports on draft evasion and study the methods described there.

647. Violate the Logan Act by attempting to make a deal with Gov. Wallace of Alabama.

648. Tell them you hate Mom, apple pie and the Flag but you love to fart.

649. Tell them you will gladly serve if they permit you to donate your pay to the Viet Cong.

Youth Dies in Plunge at Base

BOSTON, Jan. 4 (UPI)—A young man entered an unlocked office in the Boston Army Base, broke through a window and plunged to his death today, shortly before he was to have undergone a pre-induction Army examination. An Army spokesman identified the dead man as Joseph Christian Diedinger, 22 years old, of Glen Mills, Pa., who had been living temporarily in Somerville, a Boston suburb.

650. Use all the methods suggested in this book.

651. Commit yourself to a mental institution.

652. Send Peter Orlovsky in your place. Tell him to act natural.

653. Stage an elaborate demonstration outside 39 Whitehall Street, including the following:

> Six pallbearers carrying a coffin on which are painted the words GOVERNMENT ISSUE.
>
> A portable tape recorder playing Chopin's Funeral March.
>
> Four professional mourners.
>
> Ten beautiful girls wailing: "Oh where is my soldier boy now?"
>
> A huge lunkhead dressed as a sergeant, plunging his bayonet into a side of beef, yelling: "Kill! Kill!"
>
> A vial of artificial scent which gives off the odor of rotting corpses and Vietnamese fish oil.

654. Tell them you are a member of the John Birch Society and you have to stay in the United States to fight subversives.

655. Demand to be taken first at every station on the induction line and shove everyone else out of his place. Fight back!

656. Develop the falling sickness.

657. Forget how to talk.

...one group of horsemen gave me the impression of a budding rose unfolding as the bomb fell in their midst and blew them up....
Vittorio Mussolini
Ethiopia, 1934

...I watch (the pilots') hands and their feet on the controls, the delicacy of the coordination reminds me of the sure and seeming slow hands of Casals on the cello. They are truly musician's hands and they play their controls like music and they dance them like ballerinas and they make me jealous because I want so much to do it. ...
John Steinbeck
Viet Nam, 1967

Dark Recruits.

658. Tell them they shouldn't pass the Lord and praise the ammunition.

659. Have a little flag reading I AIN'T MARCHING ANY MORE up your ass and when the doctor asks you to spread your cheeks start singing it.

660. Send in a replica of yourself.

661. Bring a Holy Bible and read "Blessed are the peacemakers . . ." etc., over and over; start to sing:

> I'm gonna lay down my sword and shield
> > Down by the riverside
> > Down by the riverside.
> I'm gonna lay down my sword and shield
> > Down by the riverside,
> Ain't gonna study war no more.

For added effect make sure you have a tambourine.

Last week, seaman Weisenmuller informed BARB that one-third of the younger men at the nation's largest naval jet base were turning on with acid, pot, and some meth. Many, as a result, were dropping out of the war machine.

"As more people turned on, they realized what a ridiculous game the Military is," Weisenmuller wrote, "and what really shook up the command is when we started saying it, and (the peace symbol) began popping up on walls on the sides of planes."

Earlier this week, he said that eight more arrests at the Lemoore base brought the headbust total to twenty.

"If they break up the thing in Attack Squadron 125 there will be at least 100 arrests," Weisenmuller said.

662. Say you're a Pink Moslem and saluting an officer is contrary to your religious beliefs. (If you're Negro, say you're a Blue Moslem.)

663. Tell them there is some shit you will not eat.

664. Ask when you get your vacation and pension and if the job is covered by unemployment insurance.

665. Ask: "What if I don't like the job?"

666. Ask: "Can I get job training to be a general?"

667. Don't wear a belt, and hold up your pants with your hand, therefore being unable to fill out forms.

668. Tattoo MAKE LOVE NOT WAR on your dick.

669. Tattoo HAVE A LICK? on your dick.

670. Run into a Catholic church and demand sanctuary.

671. Tell them to go fuck themselves.

672. Tell them to go fuck themselves with a limber dick.

673. Eat shit in a dixie cup and wash it down with urine in a pop bottle. Offer your buddy (or the psychiatrist) some.

674. Stare into their eyes longer than they can stare into yours.

675. Ask them why they got those funny clothes the color of shit on.

676. Say the only corps you want to join is the SS.

677. Tell them you have a date tonight.

678. Tell them you can't serve because you have to suck milk from your mother's breast every morning or she'll be in terrible pain.

679. Tell them you can't serve because you have to suck milk from your father's breast every morning or he'll be jealous of your mother.

680. Tell them you can't serve because you have to suck milk from your dolphin's breast every evening or they'll cancel your U.S.P.H.S. grant.

681. Dance the twist continuously.

682. Dance the ballet continuously.

683. Corner the market in a commodity that is essential to the war effort. Threaten to sell to Russia unless you are declared 4-F.

684. Drink blood from a quart milk bottle while standing on line. Offer some to the next guy (or the nearest sergeant).

685. While sitting at the psychiatrist's desk blow your nose with a handkerchief which you take out of your pocket or (if nude) carry on your person, a

46. Surgeon's party

handkerchief gray with filth: snot, dirt, urine, shit, egg yellow and anything else you happen to have around. If you don't have a handkerchief blow your nose in a kleenex and then eat it.

686. Wear a sweatshirt with a big 69 on it and the inscription THE BEST MIDNIGHT SNACK.

687. Deposit ten million dollars in your local bank. Then threaten to withdraw it unless the draft board rejects you. (Since the bank president is probably on the draft board your rejection can be easily arranged.)

688. When the medic sticks a needle into your arm for the blood test, whip out your own needle and jab it into *his* arm. Tell him it's no fair unless you get some too. Offer to trade piss with him also.

689. Decline the nomination.

690. Tell them you like girls, not men.

691. Tell them: No, thanks.

692. Play a musical instrument after 6:00 P.M. on Monday in Washington Square Park, get arrested and

have a criminal record. Do this again and again
. . . harder.

693. Ask the sergeant if he has any papers, because you
want to roll a joint.

694. Ask the shrink if he got any pills cause you fresh
out.

695. Demand to make your one phone call and to see
a lawyer.

696. Have your mother come with you and sing "I
Didn't Raise My Boy to Be a Soldier" and offer
herself instead. (She should rehearse crying at
home.)

697. Set up a private espionage organization and offer
to sell your services to the highest bidder. Solicit

Vietnamese are usually slight and delicate
of stature. They place little emphasis on body-
contact sports. Thus the usual professional
man may appear almost feminine by western
standards. In addition, they have no aversion
to casual contact between males. Friends can
be observed walking arm-in-arm and even
hand-in-hand on the streets. There is no im-
plication of homosexuality in such contact. As
friendship develops, the Vietnamese physician
may extend this courtesy to his American
counterpart. However, this gesture is also a
test of response, and it should be recognized
as such. A sensible solution may lie in permit-
ting and responding to physical contact not
embarrassing, such as arms across shoulders,
and in relaxed avoidance of other forms. If an
object is being carried, it can be carried casu-
ally in the hand near the counterpart.

bids from all the Communist countries. If the FBI bothers you, respond with a ten-minute harangue on the superiority of the capitalist system, where all goods and services are sold for the highest price. Accuse the FBI agent of being a fuzzy-minded pinko.

698. Be buried in Lenin's tomb.

699. Be buried in Stalin's tomb.

700. Develop the power to cloud men's minds. Then cloud the minds of the draft board.

701. Admit you screw niggers.

702. Find out who's on your draft board and call up their mothers: "Why is your son bothering me?" Or better still have your mother call up their mothers.

703. Say you are an orthodox Jew and will not fight on Saturday.

704. Tell them they may be hanging Danny Deever but they're not going to hang you.

705. Become a male prostitute and work up an arrest record. Do it now!

706. Become an outriding Mormon: marry five girls and have five dependents, ergo no draft. Or

707. Have kids by five women without getting married. Do it now!

---

parents take action. Not all the resistance is being carried on by students. We have a copy of Vernon Jacobson's letter to his son's draft board which says: "Enclosed are the remnants of a draft card which your office mailed to my son. The card has been destroyed by the writer as a deliberate act of civil protest, with full knowledge of the consequences. Further, you are advised that so long as my children remain under my protection and support, they will be allowed to cooperate in no way whatsoever with the Selective Service System, which belongs to monarchy and to tyranny. . . . What father, seeing his son about to enter a life of crime, at any age, would not discourage him from his purpose, or what parent, seeing his child about to jump to suicide would not hold him back. I consider our present military-industrial complex to fit within both of these categories; I have no alternative but to prevent, if at all possible, their joining the common folly. . . . Gentlemen of the Selective Service, pass by my household. You are in the wrong business, on the wrong road, one that neither I nor my sons shall travel, so long as I am alive to prevent it."

708. Show up at the induction center wearing a white smock. Tell them you are a proctologist and you have been sent by Washington to inspect the assholes of all the supervisory personnel. Explain that there is a dangerous Communist spy loose and you have to find out who he is getting into.

If you are discovered, admit that you are an impostor but ask them whether they will let you look anyway, as a personal favor.

709. If you are asked to fill out papers, break every pencil or pen you are given.

710. When they give you the list of subversive organizations and ask you to check the ones you belong to,

write at the bottom (or across the list if that's the only space) that since you're an anarchist you don't believe in organizations.

711. Or, check off thirteen Communist organizations even though you're not a member of any of them. (If your membership is not later confirmed say that you used aliases when joining and you've forgotten the names you used.)

712. If, however, you have been a member of one or two organizations, check off as many more as you need to make thirteen and write FUCK CAPITALISM in big letters across the sheet.

713. Alternatively, check off six fascist organizations and seven Communist organizations and write FUCK CAPITALISM AND FUCK COMMUNISM across the sheet in large letters. When asked about the contradiction reply in outrage: "Fuck you this is a free country ain't it? I'll join any fucken organization I want!"

714. Or, check off thirteen different Communist nationality organizations such as Ukrainian Workers Society, Hungarian Peasants Club, North Yugoslav Peoples Association, Chinese-American Bund, etc.

When questioned about this, hint strongly that you are one of the nationalities experts for a government agency such as the FBI or CIA and they wouldn't really appreciate your being drafted and so the Selective Service officials should check with Washington before making asses of themselves.

715. Write out a letter saying that you are unfit for military service by reason of insanity, and forge the signature of a distant member of the American Psychiatric Association. (Use their directory.) Making up a letterhead is easy and exciting.

716. Knock at least one thing off every desk you pass.

717. Walk in on your hands, letting your shirt fall over your head and displaying your Frederick's panties which have no crotch.

718. Dye your head hair white, your eyebrows and underarms blue, and your pubic hair flaming red.

719. Take a mild overdose (be careful) of laxative the right time before and shit your pants while on line (if nude, do it on the floor). Explain that you always get diarrhea when you're nervous.

720. Carry a pepper shaker with you. On the examination line bite your nails "furtively" and then slap the offending hand loudly and pour pepper on the finger you just suck-bit.

Hershey also cutely suggests another way to beat the draft: "Join the Navy, the Marines, the Air Force, the Coast Guard." You can also pull a "Pat Nugent": spend six months on active duty and then attend weekly reserve meetings. And of course there are your local police, the FBI and the CIA (FBI agents sometimes jokingly call each other "draft dodger," a fact not without its touch of irony).

REMEMBER:
The most important thing about the war is to come back home alive!

How to produce a condition similar to eczema:

1. Scratch surface of skin with edge of a piece of glass so that red lines and scratches, but no bleeding results.

2. Grind up root and bark of daphne (see illustration below) and extract juice by pressing our thoroughly.

3. Apply juice to relatively large skin area (both your hands and forearms, for instance).

4. Repeat sufficiently. Tell doctor that you had a slight case of eczema once before, but not nearly as bad as now. Take daphne juice to hospital with you.

5. Repeat procedure when condition threatens to improve.

A.M. 11

Tough going, **SOLDIER?**

Of course it's not your fault. So, why take the punishment? If you're sick of the whole business, why not try this medicine?

1. TAKE A LAXATIVE!

2. When it has begun to work report to your doctor with the following complaints: Tell him that you had a severe attack of dysentery some months ago in Africa, South Italy or some such place with slime and blood in your motions. Since that time you notice that heavy foods, such as pork and beans, fat meats, &c., produce violent pains in your stomach and diarrhoea. Occasionally your motions have been slimy with red streaks and lumps in them. Tell the doctor that you nearly always suffer from mild gnawing pains in your abdomen high up, especially on the right side, but sometimes also lower down on the left side. Say that you feel weak and run down.

When the doctor examines you, show painful response to pressure on the right side immediately below the ribs, also during examination of the right kidney.

Stick to your story at the hospital, and don't forget to take a laxative from time to time. If you're clever, you can keep up the game for weeks and months.

The disease is *amoebic dysentery;* but for Pete's sake, don't tell the doctor that. let him find out for himself.

A.M.I

REMEMBER:
The most important thing about the war is to come back alive!

These German leaflets were dropped on American troops at Anzio in 1944. We translated them back into German, then dropped them on German troops. Aim of these leaflets and similar ones was to tell a soldier how to fake medical discharge.

721. Sing Army songs very very loudly and continuously from the moment you arrive. If asked to stop, start singing Navy songs, Marine songs, or the Internationale.

722. Or, sing radical songs very very loudly from the moment you arrive. Bring a Wobbly songbook and try to teach the songs to your fellow pre-inductees. When asked to stop, belt out "God Bless America" at the top of your lungs. Don't let them stop you until they put plaster tape over your mouth (or shoot you with a tranquilizer)—and then sue them for assault.

723. When you are tested with the eye chart, read fast (but in a broken rhythm) F-U-C-K Y-O-U S-I-R. If asked to cut the comedy and do it correctly, read F-U-C-K Y-O-U A-G-A-I-N S-I-R.

A Marine, recently returned from Viet Nam, was heard to say, "I joined the Marine Corps because I knew I would have the important experience of knowing what it is to kill. Once I killed, I realized I had already experienced killing in my own mind. Of course we have done terrible cruelties in Viet Nam but we are stopping Communism. Remember, we are stopping Communism. And an important thing I learned--was to take orders. If my commander told me to attack England in a landing party tomorrow, I'd do it without questioning him."

I wonder. Are we stopping Communism or are we stopping Life? Are we developing character or are we creating murderers? And do we imagine at the secret center of our beings that, without a deep connection with Life, we can survive merely by force of arms. I ask. I sweat. I wonder.

724. Bring a gun and a target and at an appropriate moment (say the eye exam) lean the target against a wall and start shooting at it, screaming: "Kill the Commies! Kill the fucken Commies!"

725. Carry around a handkerchief in your hand. When asked to offer your hand for fingerprints, refuse, saying that you don't want to get syphilis germs on it. When they tell you there are no syphilis germs on the ink pad, reply: "I know better," and wipe your hands with the handkerchief again. Blow on your fingers and shake out the handkerchief (as you would shake out a rug), then wipe your hands with the handkerchief again and stare off sideways into space.

726. When asked to give a urine specimen refuse to do it "in front of all these men." If given a private stall, say: "I still can't do it because of all these men on this floor—all around me."

727. Adapt all these suggestions to the *particular* situation you find yourself in. Improvise!

Bruno Bettelheim said he survived the Nazi concentration camps in this way: he had no stereotyped idea of "a Nazi" and thus was businesslike or emotional, appealed to compulsiveness or gentleness or what have you, depending on the official and the situation.

Do not assume the official before you knows what's going on in your mind. He may or may not; many times he doesn't. But in any case, do not betray your hand or telegraph your moves by "guilt" feelings.

728. Say you won't serve except as a general and ask to see where in the draft law it says that you can't be inducted as a general. If they show you the law say it's fucking undemocratic and you don't want to serve in an undemocratic army and then start singing:

One youth recently returned his draft questionnaire unfilled out & with the following notation (as best as I remember it) written at the top:

"Please take my name off your mailing list....I do not wish to belong to your despicable club. ...How did you get my name in the first place?...I have better things to do than killing and maiming poor men, defenceless women, and innocent children..."

Kuma echa sov-va-sov
Ain pa necha shov-va shov
Ain ken rosh v'ain ken sov*
La la la la

and dance the horah at the same time.

---

* No one is first,
No one is last.

Charles Neal, in his Family Finance column is a recent *Los Ángeles Times,* said that the "cost-of-killing index has almost gone out of sight." He estimates the cost of killing a man historically: In Caesar's time it was 75 cents, in Napoleon's era it was $3,000, during our Civil War it rose to $5,000. World War I brought it up to almost $21,000, and the cost during World War II was $50,000 per corpse. In the Vietnam War, ". . . the current dollars-vs-body count is in the neighborhood of $175,000." Mr. Neal concludes his article by stating, "At the rist of being labeled a peace monger, or something far worse, I predict this country will bankrupt itself in the very near future, because of military spending. It can't be any other way."

---

729. Come dressed in a Red Army uniform.

730. Come dressed in an SS uniform.

731. Come dressed in a Chinese peasant's blue denim uniform and wear a button reading I SUPPORT THE NATIONAL LIBERATION FRONT.

732. As you look for something in your wallet in front of the psychiatrist (i.e. a note from your mother which says you are nuts) let a small cloth (homemade is excellent) swastika fall out of your wallet onto the floor. Pick it up fast and jam it back into the wallet. When the psychiatrist asks you What was that? say in a low but determined voice: "I'd rather not talk about it."

733. Carry a submachine gun in your traveling bag. When asked to leave the bag behind, zip it open and shoot out all the lights, laughing hysterically: "Fuck them Commie rats! Fuck them Commie rats!"

734. Bring copies of the Declaration of Conscience, which says (paraphrased): "I refuse to join the Armed Forces and/or to fight in Viet Nam," and circulate them among your fellow draftees and try to get them to sign the statement.

PILOT STRESS LOW ON WAR MISSIONS

Study Indicates Heartbeat Average Is Near Normal

By HAROLD M. SCHMECK Jr.
Special to The New York Times

WASHINGTON, April 10—Even during bombing runs on the most hazardous missions over North Vietnam American pilots remain remarkably cool, judging from a study of their heart rates in combat.

About 30 experienced Navy pilots monitored during combat missions showed an over-all average heart rate of 94.9 beats a minute. A normal adult on the ground is likely to have a rate around 80 a minute without any substantial physical exertion or emotional stress.

Even the modest increases in heart rate in the combat pilots seemed principally related to the physical exertion of difficult flying, a medical research scientist said today.

735. Bring a defused hand grenade with you and toss it on the floor in front of the highest ranking soldier you can find. Run like hell the other way, shouting: "Die, imperialist dog!" When captured, have on you a *live* hand grenade and let them know this one *is* live.

736. Distribute free copies of *Challenge* (Progressive Labor Movement party newspaper) to your fellow pre-inductees. If anyone complains, say: "It's a democracy, isn't it?"

737. Alternatively, try to sell it to them for 10¢ and when refused, reply: "Oh, you're too cheap to spend a dime to find out the truth!"

738. Bring a water pistol with you and spray all the Army personnel you meet as soon as they turn their backs. When they take the pistol away from you (after a lecture) listen intently and abashedly and say you're sorry. As soon as the lecturer (or officer) leaves you, pull out another water pistol from your pocket and shoot him in the back, laughing hysterically.

739. Start your own Selective Service and induct *them* into SNCC.

740. Make a speech at the induction center denouncing war, the Army and the killing in Viet Nam. When asked to stop, yell that you thought this was a free country and scream (as you are being carried away): "I'm not going to die for any fucking fascist dictatorship!"

741. Look very meek. Bring along a black rosary and cast your beads in a corner. When asked if anything is the matter, burst out crying and sob: "I'm not going to die, am I? I'm not going to get killed, am I? I'm not, am I? I'm not, am I? Oh oh oh oh!"

742. Fast for three weeks before induction and tell the doctor: "I just don't feel like eating." (Anorexia nervosa.)

743. As you take your wallet out, looking for some paper with necessary information on it (such as the card from the psychiatric clinic you have luckily registered with), bring out and let fall from your pocket a loosely-stoppered vial of barbiturates (or amphetamines, or amphetamines and barbiturates, or codeine, or any available morphine-like compounds, or any combination of the above), making sure that they spill and scatter widely (better remove the stopper while your hand is still in your pocket). Gather them up fast and nervously (in an obviously guilty manner), bumping your head on the desk if possible, and mumble: "These are my medicine."

BLOOD COST CUT BY NEW PROCESS

744. If it's cold out, wear only the thinnest summer shirt and shorts and Japanese rubber sandals (pray for snow). If it's hot out, wear two pairs of socks and underwear, two shirts, two pairs of pants and a heavy (torn) winter overcoat. Undress but refuse to check your clothes, saying you don't trust the Army, and insist that you *want* to carry your clothes around with you and that you really don't mind doing it. If they try to gently take your clothes away, resist violently. When they bring you to the psychiatrist, hold all the clothes on your lap and up to your jaw. Suck on your blue woolen shirt while answering the psychiatrist's questions.

745. When they ask you to enumerate your children, put down the names of ten (if you're under 21) or seventeen (if you're over 21). Also put down four different mothers (none of whom you are married to) in four different cities. When questioned, be proud and radiate warmth and triumph. Become angry at the slightest suggestion that you are putting something over. Shout: "Do you think I'm a

liar?" If you are asked for specific addresses so that the information can be checked, become indignant and say that you don't want your women and children to be embarrassed by a bunch of jealous Army pricks.

746. Write your Congressman that a member of your local draft board is a faggot and tried to seduce you and when you refused to go along he classified you 1-A. Include carbon copies of indignant letters you have sent to *The New York Times,* the New York *Daily News,* the FBI, and Selective Service headquarters in Washington, none of which have even bothered to reply. Tell the Congressman that you feel he is your last resort, and if he doesn't answer your letter immediately you are going to picket his home.

Two Men Indicted Here For Burning Draft Cards

Two man were indicted here yesterday by a Federal grand jury on charges of burning their draft cards in a cafeteria in protest of the Vietnam war.

They were identified as Salvatore J. Bonito a 20-year-old Queens College student, whose home is in Depew, N. Y., and Ronald W. Thomas, 23 a sign painter for a department store whose home is in Cheyenne, Wyo. Both have been staying at the Sloane House, 356 34th Street.

Last March 1, the Federal Bureau of Investigation said, the two were in the Sloane House cafeteria and got into a debate on Vietnam. Protesting this country's involvement, the two were accused of setting fire to their draft cards. Others in the cafeteria notified the F.B.I.

"The Lieutenant had us move out toward the firing. We killed eight Cong and about 30 got away. Anyway we were searching the dead Cong when a wife of the one I was checking ran out of a cave and picked up a sub-machine gun and started firing at us.

"I shot her and my rifle is automatic so before I knew it I had shot about six rounds. Four of them hit her and the others went in the cave and must have bounced off the rock wall and hit the baby.

"Mom, I had to kill a woman and a baby. For the first time I felt sick to my stomach. The baby was about two months old......"

"I swear to God, this place is worse than Hell. Why must I kill women and kids? Who knows who's right? They think they are and we think we are. Both sides are losing men. I wish to God this was over."

747. Send a letter to a member of your draft board offering to suck him off if he will classify you 4-F.

748. When you get your 1-A classification, if there is a Jew on the draft board mail him a registered letter

accusing him of sending all the gentiles to get killed in Viet Nam while he lets the fat jewboys lap it up in college learning how to get on the draft board. Inform him also that you are sending a copy of this letter to the President and that Hitler was right after all and it's too bad he didn't have time to finish the job.

749. If you're Jewish and there is a gentile on your draft board, send him a registered letter (preferably on synagogue stationery) accusing him of being an antisemite and giving the names of five gentiles in your neighborhood who are not in the Army. Tell him that your forefathers came over here from Russia to avoid prejudice and that he's no better than a Communist. Say that you're not going to offer him a bribe because in spite of what he thinks not all Jews are made of money, and you simply don't have the kind of dough you heard he usually asks for. Tell him he should read Mike Gold's *Jews Without Money* and find out for himself what it is really like to be a Jew in America. Declare that you are reporting him to the FBI, the CIA, and the FEPC, and also sending a copy of this letter to the President. End your remarks with an unkind Yiddish expres-

---

According to a current joke, a G.I. in a Saigon hospital is explaining how he had been wounded. "Well," he says, "I was told that the way to tell a Viet Cong from a friendly. Vietnamese is to yell 'To hell with Ho Chi Minh!' If he shoots, he's a Viet Cong. So I saw this fellow on the road and yelled, 'To hell with Ho Chi Minh!' and he yelled back, 'To hell with Lyndon Johnson!' We were shaking hands when a truck hit us."

TIME, FEBRUARY 4, 1966

NEW HAVEN, Oct. 3 (AP) —Lieut. Gen. Lewis B. Hershey, director of the Selective Service, conceded tonight that he would "rather go to jail" than perform military service if he found it morally impossible to accept the nation's policies.

He made the statement in reply to a question from one of more than 500 persons in the Yale Law School auditorium here. He had spoken briefly on the draft system and his role as administrator.

The hypothetical question was: What would he do if he were of draft age and found he would be forced to perform military acts he "found morally impossible to support."

General Hershey responded that "in order to maintain your dignity, you'd have to go to the penitentiary."

He added that he felt sorry for anyone in such a position. "He is in a society he can't condone, but how is he going to return what he has gained from that society," he said.

(*N.Y. Times*)

sion, such as *"Zeit mir moichel—ver geharget,"** scrawled in large letters at the bottom.

---

* Do me a favor—drop dead.

750. Bring a shopping bag full of food with you to the

induction center and carry it around and eat continually even when naked. If an attempt is made to take the food away, start muttering: "What if I get hungry? . . . What if I get hungry?" If they persist, clutch the bag tightly to your body. If the bag should fortunately break while you are struggling, immediately gather up as much of the food as you can and try to stuff it into your pockets (or, if you are naked, clutch it to you).

When you are taken to the psychiatrist, disregard his first question, smile, and say (holding it in your outstretched hand with melting chocolate on your fingers): "Would you like a piece of halvah?"

751. Bring a lunchbox with you and try to take it with you on the examination line. When told to leave it with your clothing, agree. The lunch should consist of two slices of bread and a huge slab of rotting fish. For dessert, include a dixie cup with something in it that looks like ice cream but is actually shit and water. Make sure that some of the shit is smeared on the outside of the lunchbox. When they ask you about it, become very upset and yell: "Gimme back my lunch! Gimme back my lunch!" If they give it back to you, be prepared to eat a smidgen or two of shit, belch a few times, close the lunchbox and look contented. When they take you to the psychiatrist, tell him: "Oh well, you can't argue about taste."

(Or you can say: "This is a free country and it's none of your damn business what I eat.")

752. Notify your draft board every day (or even every

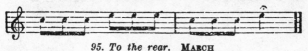

95. *To the rear.* MARCH

hour) of your changed physical condition, which you are required to do according to the statement on the back of your draft card. When appealing your classification, demand to see all the notifications you have sent.

U.S. bars medical aid to North Vietnamese

753. Fart continually, like those who are truly great. (Some carminatives are listed under "Flatulence" in the *Physician's Desk Reference,* which is available from Medical Economics, Oradell, N.J., and may be consulted free of charge at the New York Academy of Medicine Library.) If you think farting is vulgar, belch continually, like those who have truly ate.

754. If you ever had a disease, make sure you have it again on induction day.

755. Search in the *Merck Manual* (which may be purchased from Merck & Co., Rahway, N.J.) for a disease that appeals to you, then get a genuine simulated disease. Do not be too ambitious or exotic (don't try for the rarest diseases)—but on the other hand, do not assume that doctors know everything. They often know nothing about the

cause of your disease, but will hardly ever admit that to *you*. Headaches, backaches, and so forth, can have an infinity of possible causes.

Purchase a copy of *French's Index of Diagnosis* (published by Williams & Wilkins). (All these medical reference works may also be obtained from George Eliot, 1305 Second Ave., New York City.)

NB: Medical books are *not* so difficult to read, in spite of what doctors may tell you. Physicians delight in an obscurantist jargon, mostly for the same reasons any trade does; therefore you will need a *good* medical dictionary, such as Dorland's Unabridged. You will find that *pyrexia* means "fever," *epistaxis* means "nosebleed," *tachycardia* means "fast heartbeat," and *catamenia* means "menstrual period," etc. Study hard in order to arrive at the (confusing?) complex of symptoms you most desire, or the syndrome most suitable to your condition in life.

756. Be rare like Alexis St. Martin, who had a hole in his stomach, and be too valuable to the medical profession to be destroyed. Suggestions:

   1. Ford sedan up your ass.
   2. Five balls.
   3. Perfect hermaphrodite.
   4. No head.
   5. Etc.

757. Tell the psychiatrist in a gloomy tone that you are impotent and were considering committing yourself to a mental hospital or castrating yourself or ending your life, but now you are glad that the Army will do it for you. When he asks: "Do what?" say with a cackle: "Kill me!" and burst into hysterical laughter. Don't forget to express disappointment when you are told to leave the induction center. Make a fast recovery at the free clinic (if you are sent there) and then write an article for *Peace News* entitled: "I Was an Impotent for the CNVA."

758. Develop a stutter as you answer the psychiatrist's questions. If he asks you when you started to talk this way, reply: "Oh, I always do it when I'm under stress, but it's n . . . o . . . t . . . h . . . i . . . n . . . g" (take five minutes to say "nothing"). If he asks you how it is that you have no past record of stuttering, say that you were ashamed of it and that in the rare instances where it did occur you convinced the school and job officials not to put it on your record. Tell him: "They were very n . . . i . . . c . . . e" (take five minutes to say "nice").

Try practicing your stutter from the first day you register for the draft. Imagine the tense situation and then you won't even be lying.

By far the best and most comprehensive report on the subject is published by the Committee to Aid American War Objectors. It is entitled "Immigration to Canada and Its Relation to the Draft," and free copies can be obtained by writing to the Committee at **P.O. Box 4231, Vancouver 9, British Columbia, Canada.**

759. Carry a large red and black flag into the induction center, along with a portable tape recorder which is playing the Anarchist version of the Internationale. Be accompanied by a group of comrades who are shouting: "Fuck the Army!" Then start to sing:

> Onward Christian soldiers,
> Onward as to war.
> Kill your Christian brothers
> As you've done before . . .

and various raucous anti-war songs, including "Kill for Peace." When the flag is taken away from you, peel off your red and black underwear and reveal a similar flag tattooed on your chest. Have small red and black pencils concealed in your beard, which is dyed red on one side and black on the other. Fill in the even-numbered words on the questionnaire with the red pencil and the odd-numbered ones with the black pencil.

760. When asked: "Do you want to join the Army?" reply softly: "I've been waiting for a long time for a chance to shoot a motherfucken general." When sent home, mumble: "I knew you was yellow bastids all duh time anyway."

761. Learn Russian and speak only Russian. When an interpreter is called, give him only your name, rank, and serial number.

762. Learn Albanian and do likewise.

763. Learn Vietnamese and do likewise.

764. When you are in the induction center offer $50 to any inductee who will refuse to sign the loyalty oath. Speak in a loud voice and wave a $50 bill around for emphasis.

765. Offer $100 in Chinese coins to any sergeant who will spit on the Flag and say: "Fuck the imperialist United States" three times. If the sergeant takes you up on it, wait until he is finished and then say that you can't pay him after all because that would be corrupting him.

766. If you are ever photographed, expose your cock. If you have to be photographed again, promise to behave and then turn around and expose your ass.

767. Refuse to have your photograph taken. When asked why, say: "I don't want you to steal my soul."

2 G.I.'s in South Vietnam On Trial on Murder Charge

LONGBINH, South Vietnam, April 4 (UPI)—Two American soldiers went on trial today before United States Army courts-martial on charges of premeditated murder in the shooting of four Vietnamese civilians, including two young boys.

The accused were Specialist 4 Charbers Gray, 28 years old, of Warrensville, Ohio, and Specialist 4 Robert T. Tyson Jr., 20, of Vienna, Va. The prosecution charged that they had murdered all four Vietnamese in cold blood with a rifle. The maximum penalty on conviction is death.

An Air Officer Sues To Block War Duty

Special to The New York Times

DENVER, March 27 — An Air Force Academy officer, a psychology teacher until last January, filed suit in Federal Court here today for classification as a conscientious objector to the Vietnam war.

"I must stand on what I am and what I believe," Captain Noyd said in his earlier requests for resignation or reclassifcation. "The war in Vietnam is unjust and immoral, and if ordered to do so, I shall refuse to fight in that war.

Aided by Liberties Union

"The basis of my faith, beliefs and values is humanism; this essentially means respect and love for man, faith in his inherent goodness and perfectibility, and confidence in his capability to ameliorate some of the pains of the human condition."

Captain Noyd, who has been in the Air Force since 1955, when he was an honor graduate in the Reserve Officer Training Corps at Washington State University, was in an operational F-100 squadron in England for three years after he was commissioned. He received a medal for bringing a badly damaged plane down safely. He has been at the Air Force Academy since 1963.

Associated Press Wirephoto

Capt. Dale E. Noyd of Air Force in Denver yesterday.

768. Refuse to be fingerprinted; when asked why, say: "I don't want to get syphilis from all those dirty guys—who knows where they had their hands?" When you are taken to the psychiatrist, wipe the chair very carefully with a dirty snot-encrusted handkerchief, then sit down very gingerly. Stick your hands in your pockets, which have large

holes, and start playing fairly obviously with your balls. When the psychiatrist asks you what you're doing, say firmly: "I'm covering my balls to protect them from that X-ray machine," and nod at any object on the psychiatrist's desk which is not larger than 4 square inches. If reasoned with, say you know the Army has all kinds of new secret weapons. Snicker, and look around nervously. Never take your hands off your balls while in that room. If sent to a clinic or hospital, lose your symptoms immediately. When questioned, reply: "Only the Army has those secret machines—I've never found them anywhere else. The syphilis germs on men's fingers? When I screw my girl I've got no time to think about men," and laugh heartily.

769. Offer to sell the first official you meet your share of the country.

770. Keep muttering (interspersed with your other routine answers) "Fuck Johnson, Fuck Johnson, Fuck Johnson." When asked what you are saying, shout it as loud as you can. If moved on to next processor, repeat the phrase over and over. If moved still closer to the swearing-in point, convince your fellow inductees-to-be to repeat in unison with you, louder and louder and louder: FUCK JOHNSON, FUCK JOHNSON, FUCK JOHNSON!

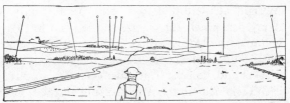

Plate 5. Suspicious Localities

771. As above, but substitute JOHNSON LOVES
     NIGGERS.

772. As above, but substitute FUCK GOD UP THE
     ASSHOLE.

773. As above, but substitute I WANT TO GET
     LAID.

774. As above, but substitute GOD REST YE MERRY
     GENTLEMEN (not the song, just the title). You
     may substitute "fuck" for "rest" at your discretion.

775. Keep singing:

     I didn't raise my boy to be a soldier,
     I raised him up to be my pride and joy.
     Who dares to put a musket on his shoulder
     To kill another mother's darling boy?

     louder and louder. Laugh first and then start cry-
     ing. Refuse to shut up.

776. As above, but bring your mother and have her
     sing it as close to you as possible.

777. As above, but both of you sing it as a duet.

778. Put on a white sailor's cap and sing "Anchors
     Aweigh" at the top of your voice; beam it only at
     Army personnel. Intersperse the song with: "Hey
     bohunk—the Army stinks." Do another stanza,
     then: "The Army was OK but it's got too many
     niggers and Polacks in it now," etc. Try to direct
     each racial slur to the Army personnel it will most
     offend.

779. Sing the following version of the Marines' Hymn:

> From the balls of Montezuma
> To the whores of Tripoli
> We fight for cunt in battles
> In the air, on land, and sea.
>
> First to fight for boobs and pussy
> And we keep our penes clean.
> And are proud to claim the title
> Of Whore-Fucking States Marines.

780. Tell them very seriously that you will start in only at a colonel's rank and salary. They will answer: "You must be joking!" but repeat yourself quite calmly, saying that this is what you're worth and you won't be associating with shits at any chicken-shit salary. Reply to their arguments in a very cool

THE KILLER JOE PIRO SHOW departs for Vietnam March 1. The nation's No. 1 dance exponent and consultant to Rowe Manufacturing Co., will take a troupe of "the sexiest dancers ever assembled" to entertain troops in the Vietnam war theater. Music will be provided on the tour by a Rowe Bandstand phonograph and sound system. Piro and company will be on tour three weeks The show should be the hit of the Vietnam circuit.

and logical manner. When they begin to get angry, react at exactly their level of emotion. But if they are sarcastic, you remain serious. Keep the tension going and repeat the entire argument logically to everyone you meet, letting your emotions rise with theirs. Create disturbance wherever you go.

781. Bring toy soldiers with you and play with them (by yourself). Talk very very slowly and softly to everyone and look away while speaking. When the psychiatrist suggests that maybe you should go home, burst into tears, throw your toy soldiers down, and run out weeping.

782. Be so ugly you fail even Army standards.

783. Be a German rocket expert.

784. Be a Russian rocket expert.

785. Tell them you will not turn your back on Alger Hiss.

786. Sing this song:

> Asshole, asshole, a soldier I will be
> Fuck you, fuck you, for curiosity,
> With piss, with piss, with pistols on my knee
> To fight for cunt, to fight for cunt, to fight for cunterie.

787. Refuse to cooperate in any way. If they tell you to stand, sit down. If they tell you to shut up, keep on yelling. If they vow they'll make a man out of you, kiss the sergeant.

788. Almost invariably the psychiatrists who are to examine you will also be engaged in private practice. Get their names from the induction center and call them twenty-five times a day. Explain how desperate you are and promise to stop annoying them if they will promise to declare you 4-F. If they fail to keep their part of the bargain, complain to the American Psychiatric Association that they have violated professional ethics. This will put a blot on their records and make them think twice before breaking another promise.

789. Tell them that you have made a pact with the Devil: in return for eternal youth you have promised to sacrifice a chicken every night at the United Hebrew Cemetery in Staten Island. You were a fool, but you agreed that if you should fail to observe this ritual for just one night the universe would be extinguished.

Obviously, if you are drafted and sent to Viet Nam you will not be able to perform the sacrifices at the proper location.

JAMES CAMERON, WRITING an admirable series of articles from Hanoi in the *Evening Standard*, describes the war thus: 'What is taking place in Vietnam, both South and North, is an offence to international decency, both disgusting and absurd, and one of its chief wrongs is that it is corrupting both the assailants and victims alike'. Adam Roberts in *Peace News* repeats Cyril Fall's assessment that as many as 13,000 minor officials have been killed by the NLF in South Vietnam. *The National Guardian* (US) reprints from the *New York Daily News* an account of the accidental dropping by the US of a load of napalm bombs near US marines in the battle of Iadrang River Valley which reads, 'The jellied, flaming gasoline—impossible to shake or scrape off once it hits the skin—splashed along the ground in a fiery dragon's tail. Screams sounded. Two men stumbled out of the inferno. Their hair burned off instantly, their clothes took not much longer . . . one man was a huge mass of blisters. Another has sucked the flames into his lungs and wheezed for breath. . . . One medic asked me to help get the men into a medivac helicopter. Tenderly we picked them up. I held the leg of the most seriously burned man. A big patch of skin came off in my hand'. *The National Guardian* further quotes from Raymond Coffey in the *New York Post*, (Nov. 19), 'Suddenly a few yards away a wounded enemy soldier lifted one arm weakly and an American sergeant poured a long burst of M-16 rifle bullets into him. "Was he trying to give up, Sarge?" a man asked. "I'd like to find more of those bastards trying to give up," the sergeant said bitterly. No one disagreed with him. Neither side was taking prisoners.' . . .

Appeal to their sense of guilt and ask whether they would like to be responsible for extinguishing the universe.

790. Tell them the above, but ask to be provided with free legal counsel to investigate whether there is any chance of abrogating your contract without jeopardizing the safety of the universe.

Propose that in case you should have to give back your eternal youth the Government should compensate you with fifty million dollars.

791. Be born again.

BOTH Japanese and world table tennis circles were greatly shaken last May when China's team turned in its biggest success in the team's three tours of Japan since 1962. This third visit found the men winning six matches and losing one, while the Chinese women won four, drew two and lost one.

How was this achieved? At a meeting after they returned home, the Chinese players declared strongly and firmly: "It's all because we study Chairman Mao's works every day! Mao Tse-tung's thought shines splendidly!"

Marines and U.S. Special Forces were forced to shoot some CIDG during the two-day evacuation so helicopters could get off the ground. One Marine said terrorized CIDG climbed aboard every aircraft that landed, clung to landing gear and tail sections and refused to be dislodged.

792. Offer the psychiatrist a stick of DMT disguised as a cigarette.

793. Talk turkey. In other words, say gobble gobble gobble gobble gobble gobble gobble.

794. Get your name on all kinds of left-wing mailing lists.

795. Join many subversive organizations. Be sure to use your right name.

796. Join the American Nazi Party. Use your right name.

797. Sign many anti-war petitions.

798. Write a threatening letter to General Westmoreland or any other general of your choice. (This may have complications. At any rate, we are advocating the letter only and are opposed to any actual violence.)

799. Get a stroke.

800. Become Postmaster-General and deliver everyone else's draft notices.

801. Become a (censored).

802. Send your Congressman a copy of this book. Ask him how the Army can possibly be putting out such trash. If he replies that the book is obviously not an Army publication tell him that McCarthy tried to investigate Communist subversion in the Army but was murdered by the In-

visible Government and we lost the Korean War and we're losing the Viet Nam War because the Army is run by the commies and fairies.

803. Never go out of the house.

804. Demand the right to counsel at all stages.

805. You have the right to refuse lie detector examination. However, you may wish to learn to beat the machine instead. It does *not* measure lies, but only your guilt responses and anxiety, which are correlated with breathing, sweating, and pulse rates. Think truth! Brainwash the machine. Practice lying on your own machine and then demand that the Army test you. This can and has been done. Vive modern technology!

806. In certain types of investigations (i.e., where you are a suspected "subversive" or malingerer), you may be asked to submit to a lie detector test. You are under no obligation to do so, but perhaps you should, due to your native curiosity about the process, and also out of a desire to FTA.

The polygraph (that means "lie detector") operator usually spends quite a bit of time—perhaps thirty or forty minutes—familiarizing you with the machine and informing you in advance of the questions he will be asking. He does this because he wants to make sure that any unusual "jump" in pulse rate, breathing rate or amount of sweating will indicate that you are lying, rather than be caused by your uneasiness at being in the testing situation.

> "I discovered in Saigon that if we do find children whom we would like to bring to Hiroshima for surgery, it would take from six months to a year to complete the official procedures for taking them out of Vietnam," the 55-year-old surgeon declared.

Cooperate with the operator up to this point. Just as the examination is about to start, however, complain that he has taken far too much of your time and you do not intend to submit any longer. (NB: There is a good reason for quitting at this point. It *hurts* to go through the test because they tie an inflatable cuff around your arm which cuts off the circulation.)

The next day, telephone the Army Intelligence agent (or whoever is handling your case) and say you're sorry you were rude, and you'll be glad to be retested. If they fall for this ruse, screw them up in the same way: go through the preliminary rigamarole and then find some excuse for leaving just before the real test begins. *Don't be afraid.* They can't force you to go through with it (even if they legally could, the results would be meaningless) and they can't stop you from walking out the door.

Out of all this you can gain perhaps the small but precious satisfaction of knowing that the services of a trained, relatively high-paid operator have been wasted, and that you have incurred the wrath of two or three Army minions.

807. Invoke the 29th Amendment to the Constitution. If they say there isn't any 29th Amendment, retort: "I'm talking about the Soviet Constitution, you schmucks!"

808. Tell the other pre-inductees that you will infect them with leprosy for $22.50 each—but only if they promise not to infect any others themselves, since that would diminish your potential market.

809. If at any stage you think your answers may tend to incriminate you or to jeopardize your position, *say nothing*.

810. Be a wife.

811. Be a good wife, for her worth is more precious than rubies.

812. Pick a fist fight with the guy next in line to you (your friend?), and then pick a fight with the guy who tries to separate you, and then pick a fight with—well, just go on picking fights, dig?

813. Be yourself.

814. Be scared. Necessity is the mother of invention.

815. Find out who is the most influential member of your draft board, and what company he works for or owns. Start a propaganda campaign against that company (direct mail, handbills, picketing, etc.), then telephone the man and promise to stop the harassment if he will get you declared 4-F.

816. Travel around the college campuses soliciting funds for Radio Hanoi.

Although few really resent the appellation "draft dodger," the migrants feel that it's more applicable to those still in the States scrambling for deferments. George S. in Toronto, for instance, still has his deferment, but he "got tired of playing their game. Getting the deferment was a cinch—I failed the written tests. Being black they expected me to be dumb—why disappoint them?" George has a bachelor's degree in journalism.

817. Start a movement which advocates that New York City secede from the U.S. and merge with Puerto Rico.

818. Be a wandering minstrel and wander over the border.

819. Use your Army papers to blow your nose.

820. Tear off the ends (a good hunk) of your papers and chew them constantly while on the examination line.

821. If at all possible, do duty in the ladies' john.

822. Ask the doc if he wants a swig (you a little drunk) and hand him an open (after you've had a shot) bottle of your piss. Have a little dripping around for obvious effect. Make sure piss is at least one day old.

823. Go on the road.

824. Bring a sketch pad and draw each examining doctor, but draw him naked. As you leave to move on to the next doctor, "accidentally" drop the sketch on the floor. Exaggerate the size of the sexual organs or make them female.

825. Send a telegram to the draft board on the day of your scheduled appearance saying you would love to talk to them, but you're on a peace demonstration today and could they please give you another appointment, which you hope to keep unless there's another demonstration that day.

826. Bring a "Tillie the Toiler" book with you and jerk off in the corner.

Plate 2. Correct and Incorrect Methods of Creeping

827. Pray to Lee Harvey Oswald to intercede on your behalf. Carry one of his relics on your person (for example, a few hairs or nail clippings housed in a silver casket).

828. Bring a portable tape recorder and play "Universal Soldier" wherever you go. If they take it away from you put up a fight and start singing it yourself and refuse to stop. Keep singing, keep singing, keep singing.

829. If you can't join 'em, beat 'em.

830. If you can't join 'em, lick 'em.

> Corporal King said he agreed with Gen. David M. Shoup, former commandant of the Marine Corps, who once told a Congressional committee: "Marines don't hate. We kill the people the President orders us to kill."

831. When you are called down for induction, repeat over and over again: "John F. Kennedy is the Living God. John F. Kennedy is the Living God." Then recite some of the awful verses of similar sentiment made up by poetasters and by hucksters who sell wall placards. Be sure to mention "John-John" with a nauseating simper in your voice. After a few minutes you will probably be so obnoxious that they will classify you anything you want just to get rid of you.

832. Enroll at the School for Marxist Studies.

833. Enroll at Moscow University.

834. Just keep on doing what you're doing.

835. As soon as you walk in, read a general anti-war statement of your own composition at the top of your own voice.

836. Refuse to be drafted.

837. Declare peace.

838. Fail the IQ test (lie about your schooling).

839. Tell the truth about all the army people you meet, i.e., call them murderers, hypocrites, stoolies, finks, idiots, jailers, moral lepers, etc.

840. Tell the truth about the wars of the U.S., i.e., make a speech explaining the true character of America's involvement in Viet Nam.

841. Burn LBJ in effigy.

No one knows how many South Vietnamese civilians have been killed or wounded. The best estimates, however, indicate that at least 25,000 civilians died last year in war-connected incidents.

842. Offer the psychiatrist a pinch of snuff, which you keep in an aspirin tin. When he refuses, take a pinch yourself—the snuff being shit, of course.

843. Fill out your draft questionnaire with ink made out of shit.

844. Fill out your draft questionnaire in manic, absolutely illegible handwriting. If it is returned with a request to write more legibly, fill it out the same way but write larger.

845. Secede from the U.S. Set up your own country and demand to be treated as a prisoner of war under the Geneva agreements.

846. Be born at home unattended by a physician and do not go to school or apply for social security or pay income tax. You thereby do not exist.

847. Keep asking each official how much you get paid if you kill a gook. Say you like the job but you

want to be paid by the piece because it encourages individual initiative and it's the American way.

848. Smear chocolate ice cream (or shit) all over your body. When asked why you did it, answer: "That's my business."

849. Bring your dog with you on a leash and insist you won't go without him. Keep hollering: "Well who's gonna take care of him? Will *you* take care of him? You want me to *kill* him—just on account of your fucken war?"

850. . . . !
(This one is too awful to mention.)

851. Admit you're a coward.

852. Drink yourself to death.

853. Tell them that Hitler is alive at U.S. Army headquarters in Saigon.

854. Ask them: "It's a free country, ain't it?" When they say well, yes, answer: "OK, I'm getting out of here and don't try to stop me."

855. Bring an expertly-crafted rubber phallus. As you are standing on line, make a great show of unwrapping it and thrusting it deep into your mouth. Move it in and out with great slurping noises. If you are naked, insert it intercrurally with a grand flourish (if you have been pedicated before, use your rectum). When questioned, reply: "If I can't get screwed by a soldier boy I have to use my pacifier."

According to a monitored broadcast, Home Minister Genki assured the public in Japan that American bombing of Japanese cities might yet prove to be "a great blessing," since it would "allow many crooked streets to be straightened and many parks and lagoons "to take the place of unsightly large buildings."

B. *Injury description:* Write *injured were*, not injured are, because death may occur before story is published.
Be direct, use the active voice.
His wrist was broken.

856. Tattoo FUCK COMMUNISM on your chest in letters 1 foot high.
857. Tattoo FUCK CAPITALISM (in Russian) in letters 1 foot high.
858. Tattoo FUCK THE ARMY, NAVY AND MARINE CORPS on your chest in letters 1 foot high. Or if you have a small chest,
859. Tattoo FUCK THE ARMED FORCES on your chest in letters 6 inches high.
860. Tattoo an American general and a WAC doing 69 on your chest (1 foot high).
861. Tattoo an American general and a Chinese People's Republic woman lieutenant doing 69 on your chest (as close to life-size as possible.)
862. Tattoo FUK FOR PEACE 1 foot high on your chest (see how many people notice the spelling mistake!).
863. Tattoo WELCOME MEMBERS OF ALLIED FORCES in a circle around your asshole.
864. Come in eating a pig's head.
865. Come in eating a dog's head.
866. Come in eating a human's head.
867. Come in eating a godhead.
868. Take $10 worth of small change and insert it in your rectum. When the asshole-inspection commences, expel the money and whisper to the doctor: "There's this and more in it for you if you get me out of here."

Artificially inducing high or low blood pressure, or smoking ink-impregnated cigarettes (to show lung spotting) are widespread measures. Getting on the attorney general's list, showing up for induction while on LSD or taking a felony rap are other gambits. A few have deliberately contracted a venereal disease. The scenes at Induction Examination Centers are beginning to approach the Greatest Show on Earth.

869. A year before you are scheduled to be called down, go to Bellevue and tell them you're afraid you're going to kill yourself. Spend a few weeks in the nuthouse and then say you feel fine. You'll probably get discharged. (If you're afraid they'll hold you there against your will, make sure beforehand that you know the sign-out psychiatrists personally.) At pre-induction, claim that you have suicidal tendencies, mentioning your nuthouse sojourn as evidence.

870. Tell them you'll go only if you can stick to a strict macrobiotic diet.

871. Keep hollering: "I want my mama!"

872. Keep hollering: "I want my girlfriend!" and weep.

873. Keep hollering: "I want my boyfriend!" and moan.

874. Come in on a dolly, your legs folded under you, cap in hand. Push yourself around and beg with this sign around your neck: WOUNDED FOR MY COUNTRY.

875. When you present your papers make sure they are covered with half-dried menstrual fluid.

876. Try to enlist in the WACS.

877. Try to enlist in the WAVES.

878. Try to enlist in the lady Marines.
879. Then, when you are inducted, refuse to go in, saying: "I've been turned down by the only branches I wanted," and show them your correspondence.
880. Become a hermit.
881. Conspire to make this world closer to the heart's desire.
882. Hide in a toilet for ten years.
883. Hide in a toilet for twelve years.
884. Hide in a toilet for fifteen years.
885. Hide in a toilet for 17½ years.

Abb. 534. Schedes
Aktives Kunstbein.

886. Hide in a toilet for 25 years. (Do not hide in a toilet for more than 25 years as the toilet will get dirty after so long.)

887. Become a civil rights victim in Mississippi.

888. Say you never voted for it.

889. Rip up every letter the draft board sends you.

890. Or, stamp the letter from the draft board (rubber stamps are cheap to make) DECEASED and then mail it back to them.

891. Or, stamp the letter MOVED—LEFT NO FORWARDING ADDRESS and mail it back to them.

892. Or, stamp the letter NOT KNOWN AT THIS ADDRESS and mail it back to them.

893. Or, stamp the letter SEX CHANGE and mail it back to them.

894. Consider the birds of the air and the lilies of the field: they do not sow, nor do they reap, and yet they are not drafted.

895. Become a horse.

896. Become a pair of ragged claws scuttling across the floors of silent seas.

897. Be a moron.

898. Be an idiot.

899. Be an imbecile, or

900. Be a Marine reservist.

901. Shut the windows and put up armor plate, leaving room for rifles to project.

902. Go to Soviet Russia as an exchange student. In your private discussions, defend the Bill of Rights and attack the Soviet one-party system. Be so out-

spoken that a stool pigeon informs to the authorities and you are arrested and tried and sentenced to a labor camp for two years.

The case will raise such a furor in the U.S. that your sentence will possibly be commuted after a few months. When you return you will be lionized and the local draft board will feel that you have already suffered enough and will not bother you.

Also, you will earn tens of thousands of dollars by selling your memoirs to the *Saturday Evening Post*.

903. Have six legs.

904. Have an extraordinarily long *membrum virile* (over 1 foot in length) which, if you were drafted, would make you the envy of the barracks and distract your fellow infantrymen so much that they would be too confused to fight. (Despite the strictures of my [TK] hygiene instructor at Brooklyn College [who used to put a bean in the jar "every time my wife and I did it, but then we ran out of beans"] that "the penis is not a muscle and does not need exercise," it would seem unjust and unphilosophical that every organ of the body should develop with use except the penis.)

A cock to the wise is sufficient.

905. Don't be processed.

Theoretically, then, it would be possible for a youth overseas to avoid military service simply by maintaining residence abroad from his 18th birthday to his 26th, after which, in normal circumstances, he would not be called for induction.

906. Say you'd rather dodge the draft than dodge bullets.
907. Say: "Why? I might get killed!"
908. Walk up to the head of your draft board, look him in the eye, grab him by the lapels, lift him up a little and whisper hoarsely: "Man, don't bug me!"
909. Get killed in Viet Nam.
910. Be your sister.
911. Be my mother.
912. Be Mahatma Gandhi.
913. Be a chipmunk.
914. Be marooned on a desert island.
915. Be marooned on a desert island with a beautiful woman, or
916. . . . fag even.
917. Make friends with the Martians. Arrange for their king to intercede with Pres. Johnson.
918. Put on tennis sneakers and a dirty skirt. Stand in Times Square giving out leaflets which assert that Robert McNamara is a Polish Jew and the leader of the Communist conspiracy.
919. Say: "I ain't marching any more."
920. Join the gypsies.
921. Find a million dollars in a toilet bowl (you the only one who dares to fish it out) and then bribe the draft board.
922. Join the CCC.
923. Join the FBI and investigate draft dodgers.
924. Join the Gestapo.
925. Become a member of the Werewolves.

94 Vietnamese Hurt in Village Bombed in Error

Fred Ward—Black Star · Newsweek—Bernard Krisher

Madame Ky before and after eyelid surgery: The better to be seen with

926. Live in a lake.
927. Run guns to the Americans.
928. Sell plans of Pearl Harbor to the Japanese.
929. Sell plans of Pearl Harbor to the Chinese.
930. Fall out the window.
931. Fall in front of a subway train.
932. Surround the induction center with paid mercenaries and take it over. Hire your own orderlies, batmen, medics and psychiatrists. Proceed to draft all those who feel that the Viet Nam war is not hot enough. Send them immediately to the jungles.
933. Be Prime Minister.
934. Eat your heart out.
935. Eat your heart and your liver.
936. Get sick.
937. Go to hell.
938. Sell your neighbor to the draft board.
939. Play dead.
940. When they ask for your name, laugh in their teeth. When they ask for your address, spit in

their faces. When they ask for your date of birth, bite off their noses. (NAPA)

941. Chop 'em to bits because you like your hamburgers raw.
942. Use magic.
943. Own a monarchy.

—photo by Bill Wingell

Cpl. Shirly Crain dug up a "Vietcong"
skull near Duo Co, named it "George," and entertains his buddies with it.

—UPI Photo

Rioters Hurl 'Assassin' Gibe At Humphrey

Continued from First Page

until he arrived back at the Crillon Hotel for a late supper Friday night.

MEMORIAL SMEARED

The worst rioting occurred ᵃʳ the Arc de Triom⁻ᵇ

944. Assassinate the Kaiser.

945. Assassinate the President.

946. Assassinate the Mayor.

947. Assassinate the Governor of New York.

948. Assassinate the Governor of New Jersey.

949. Assassinate the Governor of some other state.

950. Marry the Kaiser.

951. Marry the President.

952. Marry an African King..

953. Be a CIA man in darkest Africa.

954. Be a CIA man in darkest England.

955. Be a CIA man in darkest Israel.

956. Be a CIA man in darkest Harlem.

957. Become a bum, or

958. Become a politician.

959. Tell them you're Pius XII's illegitimate son.

960. Tell them you're Pius XII's illegitimate daughter.

961. When they ask for your occupation, reply proudly: "I'm a union organizer—and a crackerjack one too. I have great plans for the infantry. They're downtrodden and underpaid and they have no organization to speak up for them. But I'll change that, don't you worry."

962. Rent a room in the Texas Book Depository.

963. Fall down a rabbit hole.

'A million children have been killed or wounded or burned in the war. . . . Not many of them even get to hospitals, which are few and far between, but when they do, they may lie three in a bed or on newspapers on the floor. Flies are in the wounds. Even such simple equipment as cups and plates are in short supply. Materials for the adequate treatment of burns—gauze, ointments, antibiotics and plasma— are usually non-existent. . . . When "Terre des Hommes", a Swiss humanitarian organization, asked for American Government assistance in flying burned and wounded children to Europe for repair (American) officials refused. With crocodile tears they explained children are unhappy when separated from their families'. (This is an excerpt from Dr. Benjamin Spock's preface to a pamphlet 'The Children of Vietnam' distributed by Housmans in this country.)

CRIME CONTROL IS TOPIC: Attorney General Ramsey Clark, left, Under Secretary of State Nicholas deB. Katzenbach, center, and James Vorenberg, head of President's crime commission, at the opening session of the crime-control conference in Washington.

Associated Press Wirephoto

President Says High Murder Rate Is 'Monstrous'

*Tells Crime Parley in Capital
Safe Streets Are Critical
to a 'Decent Life'*

964. Buy up 100 copies of the most obscene book available. Remove the covers and substitute new ones which read: *"My Secret Life, by Lyndon B. Johnson."* Include Johnson's picture on the dust jackets. Mail books to selected legislators, clergymen and Birchers.

965. As preceding, but instead of using the innards of already-published books, write a spurious one of your own which purports to be Dean Rusk's secret diary. Make it really hot—include many references to incest and coprophagia. Advertise it in the Sunday *Times Book Review*.

966. Speak up for Jesus. When they start lecturing you about becoming a soldier, say: "Oh Jesus, Jesus, Jesus, Jesus, Jesus!"

967. Convince them that if you point your finger at any person and say *zotz*, he will drop dead. Tell them that you will be doing a lot of pointing and zotzing very soon unless they declare you 4-F.

968. Recite the *Druid's Curse* in a melancholy tone:

> May the bleeding piles assail you
> From your head down to your feet.
> May crabs the size of lobsters
> Crawl on your balls and eat.
> And when you're old and withered
> And a syphilitic wreck,
> May you fall down your own asshole
> And break your fucking neck.

969. Say that you have a cabbage patch and if they don't let you tend the cabbage patch it will grow weeds. Point out that food production is necessary for the war.

970. Become a recruiter for the Viet Cong. Offer a $25 bonus for signing up. (NAPA)
971. Burn down the Reichstag.
972. Burn down the House Office Building.
973. Tell them you're last in war, first in peace, and first to run where all the young girls are.
974. Be invisible.
975. Tell them that God is on the enemy's side and you don't want to get on the wrong side of God.
976. Set fire to the Selective Service records. By the time they are reconstructed you will be over draft age.
977. Get a letter from the papal nuncio that excuses you.
978. Register as a Communist.
979. Sell the other inductees dirty pictures.
980. Say you had a personal vision in which God appeared to you and said: "Do not kill anyone."
981. Tell them you'll bury them.
982. Tell them to fuck off.

> "As the destruction and the error intensify, so does the hatred of the villagers for the Americans, leaving the American soldier, who believed he had come to help, caught in a quicksand of hatred adn frustration. It is a hard fact for Americans to face, but it is a fact that the more Vietnamese their troops succeed in killing, and the larger the force they introduce into Vietnam, the more surely they build the very thing they are trying to destroy. The war has destroyed not only human lives but all human values as well. It undermines all government structures and systems of society, destroys the very foundations of democracy, freedom and all human systems of values. Its shame is not just the shame of the Vietnamese, but of the whole world. The whole family of mankind will share the guilt if they do not help to stop this war."
>
> Thich Nhat Hanh
> *Vietnam: Lotus in a Sea of Fire:*
> *A Buddist Proposal for Peace*

983. Lead a profligate life: cohabit with a Negro (or Negress), drink, get numerous (small) dope arrests (with plenty of publicity), gamble and also swear. Be therefore "immoral" and unsuitable for association with others in that great moral establishment The Armed Forces of the United States of (North) America.

984. Come in with a can of kerosene and matches. Threaten to immolate yourself if they draft you.

985. When the bell tolls, make sure it doesn't toll for you.

986. Rush into the induction center yelling: "The war's over! The war's over!" Hope they'll be too confused to process your papers.

987. Send David McReynolds in your place.

988. Tell them: "All right, I'll do whatever you want me to, but *please* don't throw me into the briar patch! *Please don't throw me into the briar patch!*" When they throw you into the briar patch get up and run away.

989. Tell them if they don't declare you 4-F your friends will stage a sitdown strike in the induction center.

990. Promise that if they don't draft you you will be glad to send your mother and three sisters to Viet Nam to take some of the load off the overworked Saigon prostitutes.

End-Draft Caravans In Schools

By RICHARD BARR
World Journal Tribune Staff

End-the-Draft Caravans begin visiting city and suburban public high schools today as part of a nation-wide campaign to furnish information to students seeking alternatives to military service.

The caravans, sponsored by eight anti-war groups will attempt to get high schools to teach more about non-military alternatives to war and the draft.

Explain that increasing the number of whores means that their price will go down, which will increase GI savings and help our balance-of-payments situation.

(Emphasize that your mother and three sisters are practically free from disease.)

991. Refuse to buy their program unless green stamps are offered for every enemy killed.

992. Walk into the induction center with an officer's uniform in your traveling bag. After you get your papers, go to the toilet and put the uniform on. Then go up to the desk where the papers are stamped ACCEPTED or REJECTED. Ask the sergeant in charge for the REJECTED stamp (or snitch it while he isn't looking) and stamp your papers. Return to the toilet and complete filling out the forms. Then walk out, dump the papers into the REJECTED box and leave.

993. To reduce the chances of being discovered, get your friend to dress as an officer, hand him your papers, and proceed as above. Leave separately.

994. When you go to register, tell the female clerk you want to register in the "Bugger Corps" and laugh hysterically. If she doesn't know what "bugger" means, tell her you want to register in the "Fuck Corps."

And if a prayer for the journey is necessary, one is handy, straight from the life of the Cure of Ars: "St. John Vianney, Patron of Draft Dodgers, pray for me."

995. Be an official deferred by law.

996. Get yourself ordained in the Free Catholic Church, or

997. Become a divinity student in the Free Catholic Church, or

998. Create your own church and ordain yourself its Bishop or Cardinal even (maybe Pope).

999. Demonstrate in favor of the draft at your local board. Since students who demonstrate against the draft are reclassified 1-A, then you will be reclassified 2-S.

1000. Become a card-carrying member of Kerista.

1001. Bring peace to Viet Nam: strike joy into the universe.

A SIMPLE STATEMENT ON THE WAR

Now is the time for simplicity.

The war is pathology. The masks are real, the hideousness is my hideousness, is your hideousness.

America has to hate. America needs an enemy.

Yesterday Russia, today China, tomorrow the world.

America the land of the sadist & the home of the masochist— America your Krafft is Ebing!

Yes! Pathology! & the Pathology is Sexual Pathology!

For *this* is the great area of America's frustration. Wilhelm Reich (dead in an American prison) said: "We shall never know the true place of sex in human life in our lifetimes— because of all our own distortions!" (I paraphrase.) We, the instrument, are imperfect. (Ruined? No!)

Simple ideas. Frustration leads to aggression. THOSE WHO WILL NOT LOVE WILL KILL. (Themselves, others, both!)

The politics, the economics, the ideology, the ingrown bureaucratic patterns of "decision making" (read "murder") all are subterfuge, superstructure, excuse, rationalization. ALL ARE LIES!

(cont.)

Americans want to kill! Especially old Americans. Americans in their 50's & 60's & 70's & 80's. Old Birchites, Old Presidents, Old Generals, Old Fogies of all kinds! Stuffed shirts; empty cocks.

The young get trampled and mashed in the run towards murder.

YOUNG PEOPLE will you stand it?!

O it's not quite that black & white. There are young fogies, there are old free-fuckers. America is not alone in her sexual pathology: Look at Russia yes & China: Puritans. Ready to sacrifice millions on the real altars of abstractions. Killed by symbols of "The good life." Dead for "Socialism," for the "Workers State," for the "future of mankind!"

The economically backward areas have the excuse of the anxious empty stomach, the anxious overworked heart without the materials for life. WHAT EXCUSE DO YOU HAVE O MY AMERICA?

Look look again, look in charity; none of us is perfect, none of us is the great immortal cocksman who rides across the brilliances of his life, a thousand women swooning at his bedside. All of us have known loneliness, all of us have known impotence, sexual & otherwise. All of us have been frigid before the impossible demands of sobbing life clutching, clutching asking asking for more more than we have more than we can give!

Oh America—before death crushes all the beautiful love we were created in . . . Oh America America . . .

Let us love again. Let us fuck again. Let us arise & kiss the lips of our brothers!

—TK

FOLDED FLAG

A Joyous Resistance. A peace movement that is filled with hatred is not a peace movement. A. J. Muste once said "There is no way to peace—peace is the way." Compassion for the victims of war in Vietnam must include more than compassion for the innocent children killed by our bombs. It means compassion also for the troops on both sides, who are caught by the trap of war. And it means compassion for those men in our own government who are committing the crime of this war. They, too, are victims. To attack the policies of the government is not to attack the individuals who run the government. We seek their liberation, too. The man of violence always kills a part of himself before he kills anyone else. We do not come shouting slogans but wearing flowers. We do not come with anger but with singing. The pacifist seeks the liberation of all men—including his "enemies"—and not just the liberation of a single class or race or nation.